The Regatta in the Skies

BOOKS BY LAURENCE LIEBERMAN

Poetry

The Regatta in the Skies:
   Selected Long Poems (1999)

Compass of the Dying (1998)

Dark Songs: Slave House and Synagogue (1996)

The St. Kitts Monkey Feuds (1995)

New and Selected Poems: 1962–92 (1993)

The Creole Mephistopheles (1989)

The Mural of Wakeful Sleep (1985)

Eros at the World Kite Pageant (1983)

God's Measurements (1980)

The Osprey Suicides (1973)

The Unblinding (1968)

Criticism

Beyond the Muse of Memory: Essays on
   Contemporary American Poets (1995)

Unassigned Frequencies: American Poetry in Review (1977)

The Achievement of James Dickey (1968)

LAURENCE LIEBERMAN

The Regatta in the Skies

SELECTED LONG POEMS

THE UNIVERSITY OF GEORGIA PRESS   Athens and London

Published by the University of Georgia Press
Athens, Georgia 30602
© 1999 by Laurence Lieberman
All rights reserved
Designed by Kathi Morgan
Set in Electra by G & S Typesetters

Printed digitally

Library of Congress Cataloging in Publication Data

Lieberman, Laurence.
    The regatta in the skies : selected long poems /
      by Laurence Lieberman.
      p. cm.
    ISBN 0-8203-2035-8 (pbk. : alk. paper)
    I. Title.
PS3562.I43R44   1999
811'.54—dc21   98-20341
                        CIP

British Library Cataloging in Publication Data available

Paperback ISBN-13: 978-0-8203-2035-9

For Ayla Faye, my granddaughter,
and in Memory of
Howard Moss

ACKNOWLEDGMENTS

The author wishes to thank Macmillan Publishing Co. for permission to reprint poems from the following volumes: *The Unblinding*, 1968 ("Orange County Plague: Scenes"), *The Osprey Suicides*, 1973 ("Flying on the Surface," "Whelk Hunter in the Staghorns," "Moles in the Whelk Nest"), *God's Measurements*, 1980 ("In Pursuit of the Angel," "The Sea Caves of Dogashima," "The Grave Rubbings," "Joren: The Volcanic Falls"), *Eros at the World Kite Pageant*, 1983 ("Ago Bay: The Regatta in the Skies," "The Roof Tableau of Kashikojima," "Ode to the Runaway Caves," "Song of the River Sweep").

The author gratefully acknowledges the following journals in which these poems originally appeared:

Antioch Review
   "The American Halfway" (from "Orange County
   Plague: Scenes")
American Poetry Review
   "The Sea Caves of Dogashima"
   "The Roof Tableau of Kashikojima"
Boulevard
   "Wind-surfer's Revenge at Horseshoe Battery"
The Chariton Review
   "Song of the River Sweep"
Cimarron Review
   "The Factories of Bay Leaf and Lime"
Denver Quarterly
   "Jutta, Wooing the Night Herons"
   "Bitter Faith: Song of the Lepers' Chef"
Five Points
   "Faces Etched in Bougainvillea"
The Hudson Review
   "Flying on the Surface"
   "Moles in the Whelk Nest"
   "In Pursuit of the Angel"
   "The Grave Rubbings"
   "Joren: The Volcanic Falls"

The New Yorker
  "Ago Bay: The Regatta in the Skies"
  "The Wire Forests" (from "Orange County Plague: Scenes")
Partisan Review
  "Cactus Bride: The Rain Birth of Onima"
Pequod
  "The Ghost Cross of Île des Saintes"
Quarterly West
  "Ode to the Runaway Caves"
Yale Review
  "Whelk Hunter in the Staghorns"

"Orange County Plague: Scenes" originally appeared in *A Controversy of Poets*, Doubleday Anchor anthology.

Special thanks to the Center for Advanced Study and the Program for the Study of Cultural Values and Ethics at the University of Illinois for Creative Writing Fellowships, which supported the completion of this book.

CONTENTS

1. New Poems

    Jutta, Wooing the Night Herons 3

    Faces Etched in Bougainvillea 14

    Cactus Bride: The Rain Birth of Onima 23

    The Ghost Cross of Île des Saintes 29

    Bitter Faith: Song of the Lepers' Chef 37

    The Factories of Bay Leaf and Lime 45

    Wind-surfer's Revenge at Horseshoe Battery 55

2. Earlier Poems

    Orange County Plague: Scenes 75

    Whelk Hunter in the Staghorns 84

        I. Flying on the Surface 84

        II. Whelk Hunter in the Staghorns 86

        III. Moles in the Whelk Nest 89

    In Pursuit of the Angel 91

    The Regatta in the Skies 97

        I. Ago Bay: The Regatta in the Skies 97

        II. The Roof Tableau of Kashikojima 99

        III. The Sea Caves of Dogashima 103

    The Grave Rubbings 109

    Joren: The Volcanic Falls 118

    Ode to the Runaway Caves 132

    Song of the River Sweep 156

1 ≈ New Poems

JUTTA, WOOING THE NIGHT HERONS

1.

Lionel and Jutta—
        down in their luck after eight years of sea travel
   and the *cushy* life
on their tall doublemasted schooner—
       were hard pressed to put their ship in hock for cash.
        Jutta was so swaddled
     in bandages, her face evoked Pharaoh's mummy—whatever
her queer illness or malady
   they wouldn't say.
      For these many months, no one dared ask. Poor Lionel
   was tongue-tied and wheezy-
breathed at merest hint of her affliction;
     no talking after that, a hush shrouded the subject . . .
But when she slowly peeled

                           off gauze
                    layer by layer, gossip
              buzzed around the compound: finger
           digits were missing, face parts voided, lost—
                  the gaps obtruded,
                        savagely,
              on the witness who'd try
               to look away too late. Half an ear
                    gone, or a chunk
       of nostril . . . Incurable, her illness. Perhaps
            fatal. Leprosy, AIDS, flesh-eating
             bacteria. So went the rumor
                and hearsay

mill. For long stretches,
     Jutta stayed in seclusion, hidden away, nursed
    only by dear Lionel,
  himself . . . Perhaps Lionel is the artist,
       John thought, when he hired the Aussie as handyman
          to putter around

             the cottages of the Palm Island Estate complex,
scattered over some sixty acres.
      John kept adding
            new villas to the resort: he'd leased the whole Isle
         for ninety-nine years, no less,
   from St. Vincent's Governor John Mitchell.
            And he kept running into problems with new units,
water pipes, plumbing

                                    conduits,
                           electric cables — all tricky
                  to install. Some of the subsoil coral
         was *beastly intractable*. At least twice a year,
                     full intricate network
                           of steel pipes
                  would have to be rewoven
         around the rocks. And Lionel, John found —
                           to his relief —
could work miracles with his blowtorch: a wizard
            of steel welders. The man could build
                  whole underground cities of steel
                                 tube circuits

with never a flaw.
         He could bend or curve thinnest pipes through acute
     angles; he could tie
small tubes into knots to lace your shoes,
         and never spring a leak. The recent hurricane had torn up
            the whole web of sewage
         and water pipes. In so few days, Lionel had made the rounds
with his welder's flame, fusing
      breaks in the line,
         patching leaks and replacing wide segments of soft piping
      with speed and accuracy
to match a surgeon's work of suturing
         a battalion of soldiers, near-dead with wounds and gashed
limbs spouting from a bomb

                              attack. John,
                     himself, a veteran sailor
                  but a novice in metalwork, loved

             to watch dauntless Lionel going after hitches
                   in tunnel lines. He'd put ear
                      to the ground,
           or to the tunnel entry, tap
     with his ballpeen hammer, and locate
                   the faulty links
in a subterranean shaft—whether ten inches
       or a hundred meters away. Soon after,
                he'd sweep his welder's torch—
                        a magic wand.

2.

       And thanks to daily handiwork
of such peerless quality, John put up with Lionel's
     extreme grunginess. He was a boor
           and lowlife in social manners: *wildman*
from the Australian outback whose long knotty hair-locks,
          unkempt & bedraggled, had gone
to thriving families
   of lice! His three changes of jean-
         suits went unwashed for weeks. O how could

      his ailing wife, Jutta, endure
the pig-sty he made of their home, and how abide
    all such lapses of civil hygiene?
         Her wounds perennially unhealed, sores
ever festering under those countless white layers of gauze
         wrappings (visitors often mistook
them for Winding Sheets
   on a corpse, when Jutta reclined
      motionless on a park bench)—were her hurts

     injuries suffered at the brute
hands of her untamed Aussie mate, as John surmised?...
  In time, she came forward with startling
       answers. All her body ravages sprang
from one fiery auto wreck, she the errant driver fallen
         asleep at the wheel: brave Lionel
risking his life to drag

>   her torso from the flaming hulk,
>   her scalp haloed with a ring of hair ablaze.
>
>   He covered her clothes ball-of-fire
> with his own bloodied carcass, snuffing her lacework
>   puffs of raw fire gush with his thighs
>   and flailing hands. Jutta's rescuer came
> away with third degree burns aplenty, himself . . . Today, John
>   taunts him with gibes at his shaggy
> coiffure and soiled garb.
>   *Is there no taming you, old buddy?*
>   *Do you plan to remain an adolescent,*
>
>   *or hippy, until you fetch up*
> *against Old Age?* No reply. But last week he trimmed
>   and washed his briar-hedge of orange
>   locks, for starters. . . . Jutta & Lionel
> had met on vacation in Israel twelve years back, her sole
>   trip ever away from Germany.
> Within six days, they'd
>   married: her second quick tying
>   of the nuptial knot, his first. Together,
>
>   they ran a small shop in Israel
> for three years, bought a sailboat with the money saved,
>   and set off to sea with Jutta's teenage
>   daughter; after eight years of short-term
> island holeups, *It's our last stop*, she declared. Her accident
>   squelched her Gypsy wayward soul. *Time*
> *it is to dig in. Put down*
>   *roots.* And rooted they be, at last,
>   on the Grenadines' tiniest inhabited site.

3.

> The big event—this season on Palm Island—has been Jutta's
>   breakout into painting.
>   Her close scrape with death totally roused
> her sleeping *Daemon*, jogging a latent flair for colorful

fine brushwork
on canvas into restless daily
output. To begin,
she tie-dyed blouses and skirts, vivid
uniforms that sported
local bird profiles, for the resort kitchen
crew and laundresses,
sailboat cameo
fashioned on one shoulder. Guests
from many far countries lavishly praised
the staff's costumes, and soon Jutta was struck giddy

with a windfall of garment orders, for sale to vacationers.
When the clothes furor
wound down, she took to painting animal faces
(odd curled-lip smiles her brandmark) on rocks, large & small,

which studded
borders of the one winding road
that circumscribed
the whole island; finally, she posted
jolly wooden sign-plaques
with pointer arrows at every swerve or bend
in the furrowed roadway.
The succession
of bird and creature likenesses
told a story, of sorts . . . Meantime, John,
eager to lure Jutta still further from the doldrums

of seclusion, offered her a big stack of old torn boatsails.
He'd accumulated piles
and piles of discarded sail canvas, scraps
in all shapes & sizes. Wide tall triangles. Long banners.

A few eye-
catching wild rhombuses, diamonds
and trapezoids.
He'd cut up the tattered sail sheets
into geometric patterns
that they seemed to most nearly resemble

                                 for play — no serious purpose
                                        yet come to mind.
                          But wall hangings, or drapelike
              canvas murals for decorating the cottages,
they might become — if Jutta cared to try her hand

at illustrating them. He challenged her to portray scenes
                                      from nature to match up
      with that odd assortment of raggedy shapes . . .
She began with crayons, her child's half-worn thick Crayolas,

                                    then worked
                her way up to pastels & temperas
                          which took well —
        more sweetly bonded — to the sailcloths.
            Within months, her wall spreads
hung from most villa frontrooms. Two posh hotels
                    on Union Island across the bay
                            commissioned her
            to do triptychs, wide three-panel
       lobby murals. Their managers bargained
with seamen of the wharfs and marinas, soon acquiring

large quantities of stashed-away old sails, her signature
                                  medium. In dense forest
     settings, her favorite wildlife creatures
kept peeping out between knotty trunks. Turtle. Iguana.

                                            Alligator.
          And tall stalking birds. Great Blues,
                     princely dark herons
          endemic to this isle, stole her heart —
                they'd become her secret
      passion. The week before, those seven Beauties
        hid out by day, strictly feeding
                       in reedy marshes
      at night. If you approached the gobble,
     they vanished in a great flurry of flappings —
you'd hear them less than ten feet from your footfalls,

but they were so agile and fast, they wouldn't let you
                                       catch sight of anything
          more than a tail feather-end, or a flicker
of Crown, that little white line circling the Blue's cap. . . .

4.

                        One morning,
          Lionel takes me to their hideaway retreat—
             a modest bungalow—to meet Jutta.
     It looks as if she's converted
                   half of the bedroom into work studio,
and we find her clumsily trying to stretch
               an oddshaped canvas across a tall narrow frame.
          Please don't hurry down
from the ladder top, I say,
              when Lionel warbles
     my name up to her. Distant nods. Quick exchange
of hellos. *I'll stay and help* . . . her mate
                slipping out the door, wordless . . .
     This one long banner of canvas,
        if we can get it

              taut enough,
   should match the King of tall night herons
     I visited earlier this morning,
   she sighs, tugging the upper lip
            of canvas to curl it over the stretcher
top, while I cling to the bottom flaps,
             and shoot fast rows of staples with a staple gun
          into the low wood stake.
I sweep from corner to corner,
          aiming left to right
    for best anchorage, as she instructs, then pass
   the snapping tool overhead to her, she
              poised to fasten the upper edge
   in like manner. At intervals,
      we stop to yank

and smoothen,
working for the tightest span of sailcloth
across the boards, no least wrinkle
to be allowed. *Those wonderful
long legs, unwaveringly still as I crept
up close — they must be purely transcribed!
Let there be no flaw or crinkle in my portrayal . . .*
And we each pry out
a few staples wrongly crimped
in place, drawing spare
centimeters of canvas more and more firmly
over the frame for a tenser fit. Perhaps
we're skin-topping the skeleton,
I muse, preparing it to receive
the blooded colors

of her fleshed-
out portrait. *We make a good staple duet, you
and I,* I say. *Let's stretch a few more
old sail cuttings . . . No, this one
will do,* she replies, as she sidles down
the ladder. *You're a sympathetic man, I sense
that at once. Let me share a small miracle with you! . . .
Just in the last few days,
those shy withdrawing Great Blues —
which always hid from her
before — have grown tame to her whispers. They stalk
near at her approach, and seem to listen . . .*
She pitches them morsels of fishbait.
Each bends to snap them up, drooping
gracefully to earth

from that lofty
height; or if her aim is good, they may snatch
the tossed fish gobbets out of the air
with their beaks, hardly ruffling
a feather, leaning with a slight forward
tilt, statuesque and serene — any last trace
of nervous frenzy eased by her soft call. *How I'd
love to paint one such
vertical long upreared heron*

> *in that pose: he stood*
> *there for me, without ever so much as a quiver*
> *or swerve, for a solid twelve minutes!*
> *This new canvas has the right shape*
> *and noble sweep to capture him,*
> *from crown to toe....*

5.

She'll set up her easel
  tripod in the same swamp reeds tomorrow, an hour
    or so before lightbreak—
and wait him out. *O he'll be back,*
      he knows my call . . . This said, she touches the ladder
        bottom rung and then I meet—
  for the first time—her eyes straight on. They give voice.
They speak out the *other* Jutta,
    and I catch her
      in a single fleeting glance. Knowing I've snared her secret,
  she averts her gaze, more shy
than guarded; her pupils, sunk to a depth
      beyond reckoning, say—*I've been to hellfires, sizzled*
and roasted in my shell

              like a boiled
        crustacean. Since I came back,
        all's changed. Only my art palpitates,
      my wind-bags sucking air and spitting it out—
            but for this rage of color,
                why continue?
          She has outglared death's
      feral scorch and returned, whinnying
          from every pore
  a boundless unquenchable thirst for painting.
        To daub color is her sole fury, I
          swear her eyes report it;
              she forgets

to eat, forgets sleep,
    though her paint-mind never lags, nor ever exhausts.
    But alas, her back starts

                    to give out after three all-nighters.
                        Now she winces as her heels strike the floor, freezes
                                in a crouch, then slowly
                        unbends. She points to her spine. *Just here the ache is,*
if not for my back freakouts,
        I could go on
                painting day and night, nothing would ever stop me.
                    Gently, I take her hand
            to lend support, and see her shrunk fingertips
                    scarred down to long stubs, all ten fingernails missing,
three fingers reduced

                                            to half-size
                        or less, bandaids covering
                the stump ends, sore and unhealed still.
                Her face, sporting a few gauze patches as well,
                            shows grooves of bad scarring —
                                        a few tries
                                at plastic surgery
                    perhaps, but so little original skin
                                left, transplant flaps
            don't blend well: her face a mosaic of mismatched
                    parts. Her forehead bumps and high cheek-
                                bones are so protrusive,
                                        stark outlines

show through — you hardly know
            they are covered with skin layers! In total effect,
        her face verges on the look
of a Death's-head skull shape. What chilling
            contrast with the smiley round-head face Logo, Jutta's
                    quaint personal signature
            or trademark, which she paints beneath each animal rock
portrait. The V-shaped gauze bandage
    that she now wears
            on the upper bridge of her nose looks permanent, fixed
        just below her eyes. Whenever
she laughs, as now, her teeth are the grimace
            of an Egyptian mummy exposed, its mummy-cloth wrappings
newly unwound . . . Tomorrow,

                                she's planning
                        to take the *motorized* ferry
                     South to Union Island, to begin work
                  on her two-story-high Lobby Mural. I'm welcome
                         to come along and browse, peer
                                over her shoulder
                            if I wish — she'd relish
                       the ongoing *tête-à-tête*. And *you, dear
                               Larry, may scrawl
                    notes* — O yes, those chicken-scratchy endless
                         scribbles — to your poetical heart's
                         content. And she doesn't mind
                                  telling me

(for my own good safe passage,
        so to say), that Pierside Village at Union's shore
    is a *dirty rotten little
town*, a far cry from the sweet gentlefolk
            of her Palm Island. Now some of the vagrant lowlifes,
                there, would just as soon come
            and knock her over the head to snatch her brushkit
    and paint cans as take a morning snooze
        in the freshly-
                planted hotel garden lily patch. I could, if it suits
        my pleasure, hand the brushes
    up to her at the heights of scaffold-top,
            adding *safety* by my mere presence. She'd hate to live
on that mean-spirited isle,

                                     it's bad enough
                                to work her few days there;
                           who can believe the clash of citizens
                        between two islands, so close neighbors they be? . . .
                              And I try to conjure up
                                  the scene: Jutta
                              balancing on the shaky
                    scaffolds — rogues leering, as she lavishly
                              strokes the outlines
                of her brilliant-crowned tall herons with those
                        burnt-candle-end (yes, a melted wax look
                              they do have) stubby finger
                                    digits of hers.

FACES ETCHED IN BOUGAINVILLEA

1.

               One no more reckons
      to press palm flesh of hers than to whiff fumy
miasma of a just-opened sarcophagus: to us, she's inured historic
           monument, given the full spread
           in the last twenty-five annual updates
of our Nevis Guidebook. . . . Midmorning, we arrive. Sunday.
           No advance call. We expect gateless
           wild grounds to refuse — eject us.
The drive path takes us inland a quartermile, bogs down in miry
      wheel ruts alongside a tall old revamped sugarmill,
             small cottage adjoined

               thereto. Mute, we scan
      the dim grounds, poring over broken silhouette
of a wide ranchstyle house, set back perhaps two acres from trail
           dead end. Porch eaves and doorsill
           so shrouded with cornucopias
      of wildly blossoming parti-colored bougainvillea petals
           we can hardly make out borders
           of house face through the tangled
web of vines, but gaps from lost shingles, here & there, are roof's
      giveaway as we traverse, haltingly, the secluded
           front garden. Slow steps.

               Slower. At last you purse
      your half-shut lips in the shape of her name —
Miss Wilkins . . . You puff soft greetings, soundless whisper raised
           to a cooing, then chanted refrain . . .
           No reply. *O take heart*, I say,
      you and I each shyly bidding the other to be first
           to ascend the rot-planked porch steps
           and rap on her door. But we hear
creaky floor rustlings within, and measured taps, interspersed
      with shufflings — as of a limb dragged. The door
           swings open toward us.

            We see blunt-edged cane
        poking through the door crack, followed by hairy-
    knuckled claw that clenches its curved handle, and a silverhaired
            beanpole, longboned and sleek, now
            stands before us. Balanced
        shakily on that stout cane, she speaks. Her head craned
            forward, long neck hen-quivery,
            the sentences weave and sway
    in rhythm with her ever-mobile spine. Ah, her frailties are belied
        by her grand manner, saleswoman & life talebearer
            blent, in equal parts,

            while she delineates
        her sixty-five-year saga as Nevis's ranking Art
    Laureate with nominal prompting from her beguiled arm-in-arm guests,
            ourselves. I keep verging closer
            while she gasps, asthmatically,
        between breaths. Do I fancy myself a safety net to catch
            her fall, as she bobs forward
            and back, pendular, in time
    with her wind sucks—teetering just so far, not a smidgin further,
        never quite losing her precarious fitful balance,
            hair bob thrashing about

            like a squirrel's bush
        of tail? But I never reach out, my hands pinned
    to my sides; and she stays upright, by a mysterious law of her own
            unique gravity and metabolism.
            She resembles a toy soldier
        we played with as children, oddly weighted at the base.
            No matter which way we turned
            him, even flattened sidewise
    on the tabletop, he always popped back upright when we let him go,
        shaking his sides at us with body laughter:
            so she, always bobbing

            back to cane-buttressed
        stance, no matter how obliquely angled the forward
    tilt of her shoulders asway. Oh, she finds us apt listeners, noting
            how we hang on each prize swatch
            of wholecloth from her lifelong

   tapestry of those ten thousand days of Nevis art, numbered
     as the noons of lunches, meals
      cooked, midday naps snatched —
and her works as tough-fibered and clean-scraped from local faces
     as roast pig braised & sizzled to a gourmet palate's
      fiercely exact savor....

2.

      In her eyes' pale sheen
   nineteen-twenty-five's aglow, the year she boarded
a freighter for a weekend gala first visit to St. Kitts & Nevis
     to celebrate her sister Maud's
      impulsive wedding to a Nevisian
she'd met on London holiday (she herself never betrothed,
     never *nuptialed*, to this day)....
      Now the time-sweep trolley
shunts back fifteen years more to her Montserrat toddler days.
   Her father, heir to earliest Irish settlers,
     had nurtured in her

     keen lifelong relish
   for the low-key halt pace of most islanders'
daily rounds... Her teenage years in Britain would be recalled
     as *foreign travel*, though Papa
      had meant to install her
for life in London: but those cloistered years of study
     in the famed Arts Academy
      didn't *take* — a mere school
interlude, no more. So swiftly Nevis stole her heart, the land
   no less than the lovely *downisland* serene faces,
     those peace-lit eyes

     of farmfolk and villagers,
   alike, became her best love and perennial art —
from first to last, sixty-five years of portraits true to feel.
     Her eye the constant learner,
      tutored by every face she'd met,
   she happily captured the glow of teeth and exact contour
     of cheekbones (no eye more

≈ 16

    accurate), in shades of Black
and White . . . In earliest years, local buyers kept snapping up
   her prints daily, hourly, swift though she worked
     to match the breakneck

    pace of her print-maker.
  Wait lists grew long, ever longer. But in latter
decades, the cruise ship set coaxed her to explore a flamboyant
   color palette, a splurge of colors
    to vie with the full range
  of bougainvillea blooms that encircle her gateway,
   windows, drainpipes and — billowy —
   choke up her roof eaves:
Those vines beget every petal color you can imagine — the array
  of blossoms feed my portraits today, she fondly
    declares. But alas, no

    local shop or private
  artisan can turn out good color prints by the score.
For some years, she's had to ship weekly crates of multicolored
   works to her art dealer niece
    in London, who fashions *cushiest*
  prints in quantity — twin sheaves of each chalk or pastel
   sketch: one stack bundled post-
    haste back to Nevis, the other
thick pile retained for her fast-growing clientele in Liverpool
   and London galleries . . . This year's her toughest yet,
    what with her brother

    and sister both dying
  in recent months, *sissie's* death the freshest wound —
she much the dearer sibling. Our friend, we must never forget,
   had first visited Nevis sixty-
    five years back, Maiden of Honor
  at young sis's wedding. She stayed on and on, charmed
   by this or that, who still looks
    surprised today if she happens
to recall she forgets why she never left . . . Her brother-in-law,
   sole surviving companion of six Nevis decades, still
    resides in his *Bridal*

Cottage. Just across
the dirt pathway, he inhabits quaint shanty facing
a two-story antique sugar mill remodelled into a duplex: upstairs,
we explore a small flat,
dwelling for her good friends,
blithe young couple who function as caretakers & sales
reps for Miss Wilkins' bustly
art studio and gift shop
on the ground floor below — though, of late, artist herself needs
more *seeing to*, or *looking after*, than those lovely
drawings and color prints

on display for sale!
So they report when we briefly meet, the tousled pair
breezing through the salesroom antechamber in haste to get to town
in time for Farmers' Market.
We ask after her safety,
so shaky and frail she seems. *If she'll but attend to
her walker, as doctor urges,
she'll do fine,* they cheep —
unruffled. But she's stubborn or forgetful, prefers to *gat about*
the house with her cane only, often refusing a walker
even for her outdoors

strolls. Riskier yet!
But she won't submit to constant helpmates hovering
near — she must have her *own space*. So they do keep an eye trained
on her door stoop and window
(*O please be keeping thy brusque,
poky hands to yuhselves*, she chides) . . . *Kindly wait*, we say.
*If we wish to buy a painting
or two, we'll want your services —
we'll be quick, I promise* . . . *No need, take all the time you wish*,
they reply. We're to carry our pick of her drawings
straight across the yard

to her house. Thereupon,
she'll price them on the spot, and take our money —
traveller's checks or cash, *no plastic*. And we should give her
lots of time to mull over
the price: she likes to bargain

≈ 18

   if we're choosing three or more pieces. She's a tough
     deal-maker. We needn't be chary
     not to take unfair advantage,
but today she may be fuzzy and distracted. So it's best to allow
    her to space out a bit, and she'll come around again
      at her own slow pace—

     that is, if we have time
   to spare. Ah, we do. *For her!* . . . She'd taken a fall
yesterday, bumped her head, lay in a faint on the pathway between
     house & studio for an hour
    or so. And her visiting nephew
  found her, brought her round with sniffs of *strong rum*
     spirits. She has no idea what
     happened, thinks she bumped
her forehead on tree limb, no more, and won't stand for any fuss
    about it. We mustn't be alarmed by her spaciness,
      brief fadeouts. Just wait

     her out. She'll come back
   strong, alert and eager to bargain, perhaps to tell
luminous stories about her past . . . Next moment we're stunned alone,
     left to ourselves to explore,
     in pure trust to any thief
  passersby, the hundred-odd fresh graphics: her portraits,
     still-lifes, bucolics, dozens
     hung on the sloping walls
of *Old Gaut Sugar Mill*; many more stacked in thick open-for-browse
    portfolios leant upon the wall, or piled, sloppily,
      on the one display table.

3.

     We stand upright or stoop,
   on our Honor, filing through sheaf by sheaf of works
curled up at the corners—all drafts unsigned, unpriced, ourselves
     unpoliced, and we recognize
     at a flash that we're *in presence*
  of the authentic. No bluff, no facile tricks, our Miss W's
     surely the one true Artist

Luminary of this land . . . We select
our three choice shaded faces, two child paupers, one hoary beggar
(whose age — she'll later assure us — has long since
hurtled past the Century

Mark: the wizened model
for her *Last Survivor of Slave Era,* who yet haunts
the harborside mall oft at daybreak, lives still; and by a finger
count reckoning — she taps out
the last few annums on her collar-
bone abacus — *he'll never again see his one-hundred-eighth
birthday*) . . . And we surmise we feel
her own ninetieth milestone
looming near as her eye twinkle flits, signalling she's pleased
with our picks from her gallery of local face-fare.
Not to say so by words,

her eyes alone spake it.
We nod ready thanks and yeas to the first price she,
hesitantly, quotes us for the trio of prints, no trace of a bent
to haggle or bargain on either
side. She demurely hands us
the packet of works, ribbon bow-tied in her hand's deft
style, as she unbends erect
from half-seated propped stance
on her tall kitchen stool, cane-hobbles toward her oven & strikes
a foot-long wooden match on the grindstone to light
her dormant pilot's spark.

You huddle close, but stay
just to one side. Eleven A.M. Sunday. Now she plans
to get an early start with her cooking, let the veal roast hiss
its slow simmer all day till
mid afternoon, when she'll wheel
the steaming platter on a roller cart across the cobble-
stone path to *bro-law's shack*
after her wont; and then to endure
watching the *most godawful rubbish you could dream up in a month
of Sundays on the tooobe* . . . She interjects, slyly,
the TV set's her sole

legal *proppity*—willed
to her, exclusively, by her late deceased brother.
She keeps meaning to claim the SONY portable, but she cannot bring
herself to *wrangle* it back
from Brian, he's so attached
to *the box. What else—I ask the Good Lord—has he to while
away his lazy days, bereft
of my Sissie's fuss over him?*
So she puts off the difficult task of repossession *until next week.*
Meanwhile, she carries lunch to him daily, and sits
through *Soaps dull enough*

*to plug your ears till
Judgement Day . . .* But she admits, as if we've coaxed
a coveted secret from her, a dear fine show hits *de Video Airwaves*
now and again, like last week's
best rerun: a filmbio of Hans
Christian Andersen. O how he loved—from his earliest years—
to hold forth for groups
of small children; he'd keep
their ears & hearts enthralled for untold hours at a stretch. And I
suddenly recall those bewitched, rapt child faces
in two folk renderings,

line-drawn, we've just
purchased. These children, too, as she depicts them,
may be listeners adoring that grand tale-spinner's art, but island
kid models, hairlock disheveled,
are plugged into the classic
Andersen scene retold in Nevis lights and darks, via Nevis
breezy summer nights . . . While she
chats about how *devilish grim
it be* to ferret out the rare good TV hour from the horrid program-
ming glut, putrid Soaps and the like, I drift back
to her prolific art's

genesis . . . She's fussing
over spice bottles to garnish her roast. At a break
in her chatter about Brian's *gruesome hunger for mash-em-up World
Wrestling bouts,* I ask after
her work routines, trade secrets

    of her steady flow of drawings, all of such high quality:
      does she get the help she needs
       from the home-assist agency?
O good aid's so hard to come by any more! The wound's still fresh
    from the loss of her live-in junior helpmate of some
      fifty years, dying off

       six months back at a paltry
    age seventy nine. You can't find such devoted house-
keeps today, or art-helps: the best of a bad lot, ever worse, come
      by for the few hours per week,
       charge hefty fees, but *don't give*
two hoots about you . . . Of late, it gets harder and harder
      to draw — so bleak it is to feel
       older! Too suddenly, her arm grows
stiff after so few strokes; and when she lifts her good left hand
      to the easel, the brush or chalk tip falls an inch
       too high, an inch too low

       on the page. Ink spreads
    too fast, smears or streaks. No getting the colors
right, as her sight fails — some days better than others. It's true,
      she quit reading just months ago
       to save her diminished sight
    for the squeezed work spurts. No, the *TV claptrap's* restful
      on her eyes, why it is she can't
       say, perhaps her mind wanders
and she's not watching the screen much. If the *Telly* bores her brain,
      dampens Spirit, the saving grace is it never dilutes
       last surges of her good

       .vision. They come in waves
    at daybreak. She pays out *seeing* like few last squirts
teased from the apertures of rolled-up tubes of paint. Just when
      you think color packs are empty
       (like tubes of toothpaste crushed
    to moulted snakeskin flatness), deep-dye paint globs runnel
      out, and you can spread them
       so far. *Just so it is when lost*
sight returns! What's left of my sight I save for these true lines:
    she strokes a page in progress — the moment's upon her,
      robs all further voice.

CACTUS BRIDE: THE RAIN BIRTH OF ONIMA

             Six days out of jail,
        Winfred Dania
visited Franz's class on Bonaire legends
             in the Historic Museum.
        He found himself
spellbound by the colorful maps and graphs
             linking each great myth
        to land sites
                  it adorned. More a lesson
in geography, Franz taught his pupils to know the special rocks,
      caves and pools that defined the unique landscape
of their home isle. They must never forget — the beauties of desert
             locale came first, the legends
        slowly unfolding therefrom.
      Go now, touch
      the rocks. O bend down and kiss each sacred
             stone. Become the daughter
        or sweet son
      of the Planet by embracing your true turf.
             Then study the Myths. . . .
        Franz spotted

             Winfred making sketches
on a cheap legal pad in his clipboard. He strolled down the aisle
      as he lectured to the few students, hoping to catch
sidelong glimpse of Win's pencilled jottings: no notes, he observed
             at once, but pictures — drafts
        in minute scale that caught
      the true gist
of Franz's verbal depictions of those remote
             caves and volcanic rock piles
        which gave life
to Bonaire's rich folklore. Other drawings
        portrayed the myths themselves:
      pencil lines
                  and crosshatched woven
shapes on the page captured the tales as quickly as mentor Franz

could utter them. Perhaps Winfred knew no language
but the vocabulary of pictures: luminous portraits like Medieval
Exempla. And how, he wondered,

had Winfred ever *come by*
such a gift?
When he put the question to him, he found
the artist oddly staring
upon his lips —
reading, reading, and Franz knew in a flash
this man must be deaf.
Never before
had the Museum Director
spoken with *The Deaf*, much less an earless druggie ex–con artist
of seventeen — thin and malnourished . . . But they hit
it off, from the start. Winfred, just released from a nine-month
jail sentence for heavy opium
abuse, was on strict parole,
having to report,
after class, to the Deputy Police Officer.
That very afternoon, Franz
hastened to court
to sign up as the youth's legal guardian.
And soon, the white midaged
Carib Indian

and his black phantom
alter ego had struck up a rare marriage of hearts and minds. Folks
on the street, in market or tavern, supposed Dania
to be Franz's adoptive son, so rarely were those two men beheld
apart, outside Franz's business
hours at the museum: the one
rattling off
multiple versions of key Myths and Legends
he'd collected from visits
with the *Elders*
in homes of his students; while the other,
notepad in hand, scrawled
quick portraits
of enchanted characters

≈ 24

and settings to illumine the oral texts — sketches he would later
　　　work up into full-scale paintings in oils, temperas,
gouaches. Together, they reconnoitered the sacred caves and ponds,
　　　　　　the shoreline sites and coastal

　　　　promontories, Franz fast
　　with anecdotes
of his own boyhood hideaways and stakeouts
　　　in these wilds. He'd raged
　　to learn contours,
the lay of flatlands and highlands alike:
　　　those identifying marks
　　of earth's corpus —
　　　　　nose holes, ear gulleys,
eye craters and mouth tunnels, as if the land itself were replica
　　of his own body. Or rather, those circuits of cave
grottoes had grown as familiar as curve, valley, orifice, hollow
　　　　　of his lover's body, and Franz
　　　was hell-bent to share them —
　　one and all —
with his young disciple, as Eskimo forks
　　　　over mate to a houseguest . . .
　　For workspace,
he gave Winfred free and unlimited use —
　　　sole access — to his tool
　　and machine shed,

　　　　　haven of the older man's
two decades as an inventor. Franz's secret hobby had lain fallow
　　for the past year, a time of giving over mechanical
discoveries for the arts. He turned his hand to metal sculpture,
　　　　　often salvaging the old wrecked
　　　apparatus — pipes and gauges,
　　rubber tubing
from failed inventions — in totem pole highrise
　　　　collages: Watts Towers in L.A.
　　a prototype
for his free-flying buttresses, his catchall
　　　　multistoried accretions of lofty
　　prize-winning

     mosaics. Two best tierworks
found permanent niches at street corners, monuments of the cross-
  roads, for all passing traffic — donkey cart, minibus,
fish shuttle, meat wagon or foot trekkers — to relish on the fly.
     Franz's one weak suit, his true

    blind spot — he had no knack
  or facility
for drawing, so Winfred filled this one gap
  in his repertory of talents.
  Their partnership
thrived: a top publisher of fine arts books
  in Amsterdam teamed them up
to co-author
    a first book of Bonaire
Legends; our gifted lad would compose thirty apocalyptic scenes
  to illustrate his tutor's thirty pages of text. . . .
The deaf painter, holed up beside those lathes, bunsen burners,
    pyrex flasks, wide test tubes
   & rotating electromagnetic
  torque wheels
of Franz's shut-down laboratory, commenced
  his premiere big canvas
  on the lightning-lit
night of a furious downpour. The first deluge
  in six months, it stormed
  without letup

    until dawn, while he drafted
his gorgeous tall oil painting of Onima, the historic First Lady
  of Bonaire. Boi-Nay, the first boy-man, wheedled
God in the Sun to give him a wife. The Almighty instructed him
    to hack and carve a Black Stone
  Woman, and leave her bowed
  in a low stoop
like an Olympic discus thrower's pre-vault.
  And there stood she, blackly
  aglow on rock
embankment, as a wildly glimmering night's
  electric storm pulsated

opalescence
               around her crouched figure,
full-bosomed and sultry, the stars teeming overhead; while above
       her brow, on a flat-topped mesa, stood a long row
of tall luminous cacti, clear spaces between them . . . On the canvas,
                 they seem to throb and shudder

          like animal tails, or individual
          blooded phalluses:
     one by one, those near-parallel cacti tremble
               with their own inner light.
          At first glance,
     they appear to resemble cactus picket fences
               which surround and protect
          old Plantation
                    Estates, scattered here & there
throughout the island. But those other ranks are static legions
     of the living dead, while these furry pricklers hover
in place, a spiritual congregation of cacti standing in chorus
                 under an explosive starry sky.
          They shriek their happy news
     to the Heavens!
     The birth of Boi-Nay's mate. The first woman
               hunkering on the rock below.
          Look, she is open
     to the night's electric showers. She drinks,
               drinks of the cactus outflow. . . .
          O how Winfred

               must have struggled to control
those bold wavery cliff lines, as well as that woman's upraised
     arms and rotund shoulders. Three days of heavy rain
drove the humidity so high, the supple paint stayed damp: colors
               streaked and ran. Multiple figures
          of woman and cactus sentinels
     kept rippling
and softening in outline, while the artist
          bolstered them with primary
     color source.
     Winfred lost count of how many paint layers

              it took to make the cactus
        rinds becalmed,
                    no reprieve until the gush
of rain subsided. He never slept, ate or drank until the paint
        dried, his vigilance needed every minute to guard
the painted shapes . . . Skies cleared. He stalked into the light
                to view his cactus bride.

THE GHOST CROSS OF ÎLE DES SAINTES

1.

Nigel and Dan, on holiday from the State Department, both
        fluent in French,
           take a fancy to ourselves.
   Do let's join forces, saith Nigel; all agreed,
  we four team up in a one day car rental. Nigel roars
South at a fierce clip,
        arriving at Trois Rivieres a full hour early
        for the commuter shuttle.
     We fall prey, at once, to vile hawker reps
for three competing ferry lines — who haggle us
    to patronize their craft, most punctual
    and speedy. But we opt aboard

the slower vessel . . . Last-minute plan switch. Nigel prefers
        a whole day solo
          drive in Guadeloupe, minus
   companions, we to join Dan on foot trek search
  across *Île des Saintes* for reclusive local sculptor
of note: Jerome Hoff
        (idol of Dan's art collector friends in D.C.),
        armed with a few scrawled road
        jottings on a half page of notepad — for map. . . .
Day overcast. Storm clouds darkening overhead.
   A curb to direct sunblaze, at last,
   your first chance to dispense

with layers and layers of sunblock, sea spray fast thwacking
        our half-bare skins
          in flashes, as this antique
  fish sloop axes breakers with its cutting bow;
  sky gush erupts, hard rain no threat, it's all the one
wetting . . . Mist lifts.
        We dock on *Saintes*, go off on foot for our day's
        wayfarings, no rental cars
        or vans. And what a difference to size up

a lovely curvaceous sweep of island, *eye gauge*
    those dramatic vertical and horizontal
    hike miles we can weigh,

purely, against our rigor of bone and muscle reserves: both
    isle extremities,
        East & West, visible at once,
the hilltop Fort Napoleon's tower and flag
so many foot kilometers above, and we smile at hike
prospects. Dan leads.
    Our sculptor's den, we're told, is halfway up
    the undulating paved ascent
    to the Fort—a shallow dropoff at roadside
on the Carib Sea overlook. As we climb, I keep
    nabbing best views of hills and rooftops,
    then gasp at tall White Cross

that looms into view, starkly aglitter, between two hill peaks.
    The horizontal beam
        seems to shudder, wildly fluctuant
like a massive windmill's flat propeller blades.
Phantom Cross, itself, appears to twist or oscillate
and not ourselves, who keep
    turning to face blazing White Holy Stanchion,
    the light shimmer oddly enhanced
by sky's overcast. We behold no breaks or gaps
in cloud bank—hurled spears of light seem sourceless,
    the towering Cross apulse with heat flashes.
    Wildfire of mute lightning . . .

2.

        Absently, I tumble
    into Hoff's doorwell, his sunken entryway
        oddly close to the much-trafficked
            road edge. *How,*
    I wonder, do those scads of teenagers
        racing motorbikes,
    or tourists in jeeps and mokes
        straddling the shoulder, avoid grazing
    his gates & doorpost? The bungalow, set down

                    from the road a few steps, seems ashen gray dusk
                    after sheen of dayglare —

we duck our heads, chary as a team of spelunkers
entering a cave mouth. Just inside
the doorstoop, we're regaled with a passage
of scripture, half-sung and half-
recited in French,

                    as if each day's
welcome be snared from a fresh patch of Hoff's
                    Biblical text. Long pale streaks of light
                            meshed with shadow
            bob and flicker on the wood-panel ceiling,
                    shrunk candle wick
        fallen low in its guttered-down
                    puddle of melted wax upborne in a saucer
        shakily balanced on the outstretched palm
                    of our host, whose cautious *Who cometh?* explodes
                    into great friendly squawks

and hurrahs, at our softly naming the mutual friend
in D.C. who sent us to Île des Saintes
to fetch for transport home three prepaid Hoff
sculptures (lightweight, Dan hopes,
travelling carry-on

                    and backpack light
himself) . . . Glad repartee is bandied to and fro
                    so swiftly between them, I half miss
                            French niceties
        and key details, until Dan's relief erupts.
                    The commissioned works,
        yet incomplete, have fallen behind
                    the promised schedule (indeed, whose High
        Art can ever be bound to fixed time limits?),
                    Dan to be spared the task of lugging those treasures
                    back to the States: no fault

of his own . . . Hoff finger snuffs his low candle's wick
and throws open two wide sets of shutters
(he'd been napping when we knocked, as rumpled

bedclothes on the rear floor pallet
quickly reveal),

                his arms outswung
      ever wider, as if to embrace both ourselves
                     and inrush of light from those windows
                        fiercely aglow.
                And he belts out seven or eight booming *Kyries*,
              one after another,
         without pause to draw least breath —
                      most prodigious wind control, operatic
and devotional at once. How well we know we're
           in presence of a princely vocalist, one endowed
        with great laryngeal thrust

to shore up the rear in any thin-voiced school chorus
or civic holiday ensemble. We burst
into applause, following the last rafter-
wobbling *Kyrie*. . . . For thirty years,
since he first broke

               away from the ranks
of gifted boy sopranos, and became this Isle's
          lead tenor, he'd held forth without fail
              in Church Choir,
     his voice never once lapsed from weekly service.
        A soul totally driven
    to mould visions in woodcraft & stone,
                this man remains ensconced — unwaveringly —
in village Church Mass. And now to hear him speak
            of the choiring young & oldsters wedded in litany
        you'd think that Art of Voice

were his first joy, all the while he extols the choir
master's many tireless rehearsals,
each week, to make those diverse voice timbres
commingle in perfect blend.
Short of stature,

             a tad roly-poly
but not stout, Hoff's beefy redveined nose, cheeks

and furrowed brow are hotly inflamed
with his discourse . . .
Glancing, repeatedly, at the overhead shelves
stacked from cabin wall
to wall with his own last season's glut
of wood sculpture, I'm reminded that Hoff's
less your vocal stalwart than master of blocks,
lumps, tubes, slim wands or fat clubs of fresh-hewn
tree corpus. Devout lover

of the pine or cedar limb's sweet veins, knots, forks
& contours. He sees my stunned eyes flit
from statue to moulding, then from upright Saint
to those sprawled prostrate Sinners.
But for the moment,

he deflects my art
queries, and launches into a chronicle
of star-crossed family history.
Oh, he finds us
apt listeners — we hearken after tales
of his ten siblings
and himself, all third generation
native West Indians. Their ancestors,
in mass exodus from Alsace-Lorraine, hied
themselves — a race to escape German war threats
at Franco-Prussian borders —

to remote Guadeloupe and its sister islet, *Saintes* . . .
Despite local fame of some years, our host
has never journeyed from these French Antilles'
cramped shores, whether for study, play,
business or Art. . . .

3.

To hear the word *Art* starts
my eye to clandestine rovings of the half-darkened upper
wallspace above the top tier
of four shelves crammed with recent sculptings.

And now, I'm startled by blonde frames of scattered
paintings, oil on canvas, hung
at high levels near the ceiling, mounted well back
from far more numerous works of wood & stone.
Looking closer, I observe that all oils —
in whatever size or colors —
are strikingly inferior to the sculptures. So they recede

into backdrop by quality
as much as by remote placement in recesses of the room's
two corner alcoves. Subjects
and motifs on canvas, though near identical
to the sculpted figures, lose depth and amplitude:
a flattened-out medium,
color range diluting — nor yet enlivening — the impact.
This man should keep to shapes moulded in space,
all his genius freed by the flakes chiseled
or hacked from wood hunks
and slabs of stone, much as those chips & shavings from two works

in progress on a workbench
below the shutters flung open moments ago . . . I dare not
divulge my paltry cavilings
at Hoff's draftsmanship or colorist technique,
not even by my unguarded eye shifts from woodblocks
to canvas and back . . . O Hoff
spots my drift, my wavering from his euphonious
monologue and drawlings upon family sagas;
quick, before he can suspect me of worse
default than sheer love
of woodcraft, I blurt my true ardor for those stately twin oak

carvings on the lowest shelf:
I'm thrilled by those two beauties! One, a child propped
on that bearded thin fellow's
left shoulder. The other, a near-match for size
& stance, while the child, spread-legged, straddles
both shoulders. Are the subjects
your tall brother and nephew of whom you just spoke —
family portraits?, I ask, hoping to score marks
for good faith by the chance intertwining

≈ 34

            of his garrulous family
chronicle and my quick pix of his lovely Art's high water marks.

               Then, I make my thirsty most
         of the pause—while Dan translates my bold Anglo question
         into passable Creole French
     for our host—and give my full unfettered glare,
    at last, to shelved wonders lining all four hut walls.
  Most are tall standing figures,
   whether sculpted from stout oaken blocks or random
    street finds—clubs, old furniture discards,
  driftwood posts; large pieces interspersed
        with close-detailed carvings
on narrow shafts: knotty walking stick, thin cane, old broom handle,

            soccer paddle, canoe oar . . .
      My eye bristles at the challenge to unlock secret origins
     in a breathless succession
    of novel *found* objects, mostly throwaway sticks
     from backalley and household resurrected for a second
  life on Hoff's blessed shelves,
  so many destined, I feel, for more permanent homes
   in gallery, museum or art collector's nook . . .
Great bursts of hilarity, coming in waves
      like uncontrollable sneezes,
disrupt my trance of poring over the statues, while Dan translates,

          in reverse, Hoff's amazed
      response to my Biblical naiveté. *Never* his dear family kin,
      his art pilgrims—as always—
   are Heroes & Saints lifted purely from Scripture.
    The twin pairings of man and shoulder-bestrid infant,
  so far removed from Hoff's brother
 and nephew, are both versions in his ongoing sequence
 of tributes to St. Christopher, the patron saint
for travellers, carrying a child to safety
      from siege of war or storm—
one leg upraised, the other swept back, as he lunges through fire,

         hurled missiles, severe wind
      and hail . . . Yes, now I can see the legs are indeed lifted

        in mid prance, at full stretch,
           but difficult to make out in the narrow confines
      of lean sculptured wood pipes. I redden, my blunder
    exposed. Not prone to shame me,
      Hoff's taken my blind misreading of Christian Ikons
        as occasion to inquire after our own key church
    affiliation, Dan then translating our reply—
           if imprecisely—as *Hebrews*.
Oh how can that be?, Hoff frets, pity and horror sweeping away

        all measured view of ourselves.
      Standing perplexed and tongue-tied, he visibly cogitates
        over our strange forced exile
    in the United States, since we *must* be citizens
      of Jerusalem fled, for obscure cause, to dim hermitage:
        pained refuge in that country
    of the filthy-rich oil barons and family betrayals
      rife on such TV sagas as *Dynasty* and *Dallas*,
        his favorite Soaps that he takes as Gospel
           and true mirror of American
lives. But no, we are Jews, Jews simply, and not native Israelis.

        A parochial class harbored,
      today, by all modern nations. But he urges me to take heed,
        great heed, for we're *in danger*.
    So pungent his dread, I glance back over my shoulder
      for would-be assassins. Dan calms our holy guide & mentor,
        then our unsavioured selves.
    Our peril, though imminent, is otherworldly! No physical
      threat, nor a recurrence of Nazism—gas chambers,
    mass incinerations . . . We must beware our Souls'
        shaky footing in the life
to come. May his Art, he prays, light the true *hereafter* for us.

≈ 36

BITTER FAITH: SONG OF THE LEPERS' CHEF

I.

Disguised with fake names
like *Quarantine Hospice* or *Contagious Retreat*, the last hangers-on
    Leper Colonies persisted into the fifties and sixties,
a well-kept secret never to be hinted to visiting Heads of State,
              on pain of. . . . In backwoods
        St. Maarten and Guadeloupe,
    those hideaway
ruins lumped together the widest spectrum
        of incurables — more detention
        camp or jail
than healing ward. Dying or brainsickly
        or crippled, scores of folks
      might be herded
                into barracks: a fort ruin
or desolate old church the main headquarters, but sprawling Tent
    Cities would radiate outwards like spokes of a wheel
to take up the slack, whenever numbers soared . . . Most infirmaries
                of the damned — repulsed Souls —

            dwindled and fell away
by turn of the Century. But some few lingered obscurely, decade
    after decade — the dates are muffled, so many layers
of secrecy and denial cobwebbing the facts. A few last straggler
                victims eked out a famished
        survival, long after reported
      site closedowns . . .
    Families living near the infamous *estates*
        shun the environs, for fear
      that never-ending
contamination of floors, walls, doorsills
        has spread to outlying grounds.
    All dark rumors
            are true, says Françoise,
as we drive up the pathway to a deserted fort behind Sandy Point
    township. *Here, in the St. Kitts outback, one leper's*

hermitage survives to this day. On recent maps, this musty ruin
never shows up. There's no sign

it's slated for facelift
or renovation, unlike most historic sites. Some fourteen lepers,
many in advanced states of decrepitude, still haunt
the interior. Pallet straw mats on cubicle floor for bed, inmates
rarely step outdoors, at least
by day — they fatuously wander
the blank canteen,
cramped barren stairwell and unlit corridors,
none wired for electricity.
Meager funds
for candles ran out, the compound blotted
from the City Manager's
shallow memory,
though private charities
often send in foodstuffs, old clothes mended.... The resident cook,
that one trustworthy caretaker, meets us at the gate
on the appointed hour for *guest visits* — rarely family or friends.
(The stayalive troupers, stubborn

ghost-clingers-to-life-
by-a-thread, long since banished from all ties to Kin or Beloved,
it's only gawkers and meddlers, yes, like ourselves,
who come to pay their hollow respects... *And pay alms, Pray God.*)
No phones to call ahead, we're
untimely and intrusive, at best.
Hyacinth, tall
broad-shouldered Asian garbed in wraparound
white apron — neck festooned
with ribbon
crossties and wavy collar — blocks our passage,
wielding a shiny butcher's
cleaver. We waft
the Magistrate's Seal
under her nose — authorizing our visit. But do we know the risks
of consorting with the inmates, whose close relatives —
grandson, aunt, nephew or brother — wear gauze face masks, veils,
rubber gloves perhaps. Indeed,

                    what can be *our* Mission?
Purportedly, she's chased away scores of thrill-seekers, gloaters
        hunting a freakshow, with her plague threats and scare
tactics. Are we daredevils, missionaries of a High Faith, philan-
                        thropists? Or students in search
            of Truth of forgotten lives,
        those abandoned —
    or unfairly banished — Souls trapped within?
                Françoise, a Museum Curator,
            social activist
    and crusading champion for human rights,
            rights of neglected *undying*
        sick paupers. I,
                    a writer of verse . . . We'll
    pass muster, her eyes signify. And she gives us the nod to stroll
        through the gates, soon to chance upon Chester quietly
fashioning a clay flagon at his potter's wheel in open courtyard.
                A dozen ceramic vases and bowls

                and mugs, fully glazed,
line a shelf behind him. A kiln looms beside the near wall. He wears
    thick raggedy leather gloves, and rising to greet us,
he shakes hands with his gloved two fingers — thus making a big point,
                unspoken, of keeping that sheath
        of insulation between our skins.
            Now he speaks
        visibly to one side of our faces, so to screen
            us from his possible voice spray.
        Gallant gestures,
            these token safety tactics, though our friend
                in Basseterre — Chief Minister
            of Health — assured
                    us, there's no real danger
of contagion here. The phase of passing on the virus, or infectious
    microbes, is *kaput*, in all cases. We are invulnerable,
or immune, since leprosy thrives on total voids: no vitamin surplus,
                poor sanitation & waste disposal.

                So we may safely ignore
the warnings. House staff are guarding privacy, not public health,
    for all the palaver about quarantines . . . Chef Hyacinth

resumes our tutelage and walkabout of near-lightless inner chambers.
                    Her illness, stalled in remission
            at an early stage of symptoms —
        if no less
    lethal than most — is the rarer *dry leprosy.*
            She confides to us, in hushed
                undertones,
        that her flesh-gouging damage is internal:
            the horrible *eatout of tissues*
        will stay hidden
                        until those final weeks
before dying. Then great blisters, popping like volcanic geysers
    and jets, shall reveal to the eye all deep scoopouts
of muscle and cartilage, a circuit of gaps in thigh and leg-shank
                and buttock, as if some demonic

            icecream scooper had dug
regular spheroids of flesh mounds, leaving many never-to-be-filled
        sockets in their place. For years, as the inner fissures
deepen, the victim may appear to be whole and intact, outwardly;
                but a decided limp or careening-
            to-one-side style of locomotion
        often ensues,
    while the concealed pockets cave in, or rupture.
            The unsuspecting walker, atilt,
            improvises
        radical new modes of balancement to help offset
            or compensate lost body zones.
        So far, Hyacinth
                    exhibits no overt sign
of this queer malady. She knows she's been stricken, beyond cure,
    but the disease may stall out, hanging fire for years
in remission . . . All other lepers in the Fort Compound, she notes,
                are cases of familiar *Wet Leprosy.*

II.

    Now we take muffled short steps down
                the long fort corridor,
            stopping at a series of closed

cells, each in turn.
We knock
at thick hardwood doors,
then encounter the occupants, all
missing fingers, hand parts,
or even elbows —
but faces,

happily,
intact. Eager
to meet us they are,
and bristling to tell grim sagas
of their family
expulsion.
Two young women, still
in their thirties, cling to a wish
that their parents, or
Great Aunt, will — one day — welcome them

back from exile. Back from this horror
of pre-death, a premature
burial . . . Two factions, consigned
to far-flung wings
of Castle,
sport widely differing
wounds: both missing overt body parts,
both of the *wet* garish eyesore
type; to one degree
or another

viewed as
monsters or fiends
by the unfeeling public.
Our two lady confidantes belong
to the less severe
breed, who
sustain all body
deletions — all loppings away,
falloffs in the night —
in the appendages. At the grim onset,

finger digits and toe parts may unhinge;
knucklebones & small wrist
flakes are next to erode, dissolve,
or moult like snakeskins.
Later, toe
or finger segments,
unbloodied and unfrayed, will show up
beneath pillows, or tangled
in loose bedsheets
perhaps . . .

Though slim
and hollow-cheeked,
their sweet faces are cameos
of taut beauty: no damages endured
above their necks,
no gash
inflicted on cheeks
or brow. But O how amazed they
still are — each recounts —
when small flesh slugs disengage, oddly,

from hands or feet — at chance moments
of wakeup from light sleeps.
Often, they are given to frenzied
snatches of fallen
members,
and futile attempts
at patchup or reassembly. Last week,
chants Abigail, she struggled
to sew back in place
three fallen

toe stubs
with surgical black
threads, cutting the healthy
tissues at the joint or break sites —
in hopes fast gush
of serums
enhance a fresh seal
by some miracle of quick-healer

                    coagulants. No use, ever . . .
                    Now Gladys, in raw moments of baring all,

reveals a cleft in her forearm where one
              wrist has begun to dislodge.
         She, following a young paramedic's
                    advice, undertook
                       a program
                 of daily weight-lifting
        routines, thereby to rebuild flaccid
           muscle and cartilage. Her hand,
                as we can make out,
                     half-dangled

                          half-bobbing
                          and quivery, yet clings
                          to its main branch of tendons,
                          veins, artery as a peninsula of land
                          connected by narrow
                          isthmus
                          to the mainland defies
                          joint assault of heavy surf, razing
                          tides and typhoon to banish
                          it to an island exile . . . But worst case

lepers, confined to those remotest cells
            in the Fort's upper stories,
hide in dark corners — face & skull
              parts cruelly gouged
                   by a savage
           microbe God. They refuse
     to be seen by anyone but their fellow
        amputee grotesques, even glaring
                at Chef and helpmate
                    Hyacinth when

                          she arrives
                          with the supper tray,
                          or retrieves the shit bucket.
                          She waves her thumbless two-fingered
                          swollen-knuckled HALF

     FIST at them,
     and makes her mute claim
     to ranks of the slow-devoured bods.
     Most days, they abide *her*
     but no outsiders, too ashamed — or is it

strangely proud? — of their deformities . . .
    Half a nose sloughed off,
  or three fourths of a chin mushed
     into a pillow this A.M.,
      the waker,
    thinking he spat up
last night's mutton stew, soon learns —
to his horror — it's jawbone & jowls
    sloshed on the coarse
     bed sheets!

     No way
     might he have guessed,
     from the texture of fallen skin
     glop, whether these be cartilaginous.
     Bewildered, he'll trace
     the new gap
     in his lower face
     with a groping fingerend. Likewise,
     a tooth dispelled in sleep
     may show up, first, as an unfamiliar pit

to tongue tip's desultory waggle, before
  fallen husk of decayed enamel
  slips from the twisted bedclothes.
      But no tooth-fairy's
     silver coin
    shall reward *this* sleeper
for lost eyelid, nose tip, lip or gum
  segment brushed under a pillow
    in the night. O sighs
     upon waking. . . .

THE FACTORIES OF BAY LEAF AND LIME

1.

To this day,
limes be still de prime leaf of Montserrat's Shamrock Logos
    proudly displayed
  on flags, pennants and bumper stickers: everpresent!,
   says Thomas. . . . A few hundred meters up the road
from eviscerated corpses of old-soldier lime distillery
    boiler tanks
  abandoned in a wayside ditch, we roll, bumpily,
    down cobblestone

                              paved sidepath
    midway between two factories, both going enterprises.
               What a contrast,
  I think, between the foursquare boxy Emerald Brewery—
    which bottles local beer and native mango rum
Spirits—and the big old two story country plantation house
                      converted
    to a multifaceted boilerworks. How amazing,
         the lengths to which

local veteran
architects have gone to design and improvise a homemade dual
    research lab
  and factory from the warped husk of this one historic
    Greathouse: some wall units torn out, others
fitted with barrels—half in, half out of the chambers; pipes
    and meters,
    gauges, little chimneys protruding at odd angles
      from knotholes, slots

                             and wider gaps
    punched through this antique mansion's rickety wall panels.
               As we approach
    our conjoint villa and refinery all rolled into one
    huffing and chugging gasworks, assembly plant,

Lord-knows-what, I'm dizzied by a blast of smoke fumes: green-
gray billows
rolling over me from two or three chimney pipes,
smokestacks in a roofless

back gallery.
I wait for the wind to shift, the fumes thinning enough for me
to breath easy.
*Yes, my friend, now I'm ready. Let us proceed indoors—
is this acidic fragrance scent of burnt limes,
lemons, neither quite, but something similar?* Thomas, in lieu
of reply,
exhibits his limpid smile: *Come see for yourself.*
We bypass front doorstoop

and vestibule,
circling about to the right, where the action is in progress,
sparks and flame-
flickers emanating from a tall cube shape: incinerator
or outdoors furnace, wide stovepipe overhead
coughing and spitting the aforementioned gases . . . High-pitched
sighs of ardor
greet us — the happy timbre of a matronly woman
precedes her full-bosomed

ample carriage
and outstretched arm of welcome. She embraces Thomas's neck
with her forearm
and playfully tweaks his chin (sometime lovers, these two,
my fleeting guess), all the while her left arm
works machine lever up and down, paced in tempo with her foot
kicking stubborn
pedal, a bit jammed, but no match for her adamant
will and burly stomp.

Prompted by Thom's
hidden nudge in my vertebrae, I take a few wary short steps
toward Luella's
steamy work space. One leg sinks in a spongy morass,
my other leg slipping on slick floor boards
before I can grope for balance, both hands wildly flailing

≈ 46

                                    at supportless
              air, when she clasps my wrist and draws me slantwise
                                  to a zigzag walkway:

ramshackle bridge
across the mush sinkhole underfoot. Now stabilized on two boards
       of the piecemeal
    footpath, I note I'd been poised to wallow in that sea
    of yellow-gold crushed lime rinds, bottomless
    layers of thick lime husks, when she shooed me onto those planks,
       cooing: *Take care,*
       or you'll sink in dem quicksands of moshed lime crud.
       Next, Luella turns her back.

                                   Swift maneuvers.
   Two boiler machines slowed to idle, both placed on hold; other
                                sizzling gizmos
        shut off; the tallest rumbly barrel revved up, then left
              on automatic pilot. At last, she hand waves
us to the back garden. I follow her to a dense-leafed low shrub,
                              wherefrom she plucks
          three small green fruit from limbs just overhead,
                        crosses my palm with the gift.

Wild tangy limes.
At her cue, we approach a pair of taller broad-leafed saplings,
       quick she snaps
    wide leaves from low-hung stems, fixes one in my shirt
    lapel like a carnation and crackles the others
    beneath my nostrils: what a kicker!, those bay aromas so fierce
       my sinuses burn
       and prickle. . . . *Tell us the formulas,* Thom whispers,
       for your own unique blend

                                           of de bay oils,
            awarded, four years running, first prize for duh tart flavour
                                    and pungency.
             No way, she replies. *Ah cain't reveal de close-moufed*
                          secrets of me trade, don't you know. I turn
         away, thinking we've overstayed our brief welcome, but Luella
                                     tugs my elbow

        back to her burbling stills, her face open and gay,
                eager to come clean,

to divulge all.
She affixes a thin rubber hose to the tall glass demo bottle,
    twists the tap
      and catches in a cup the juice that flows from the tube.
        Two cloudy masses, above and below, approach
    each other, while the pure clear juice in the middle drains out.
        She offers me
    a sniff, then a sip—no mistake about it, freshest
      lime juice I've sampled,

                            sour and piquant.
    She fills the cup and shuts the faucet, a few spurts of overflow
                droplets trickled
on the floor. She points to the murky areas, mere smidgin
        of fluid left between them: two rich sediments,
varied in color and mass, they form the base medium for lime oil.
                    One cloud sinks.
    The other floats. A thinnest layer—that immiscible film
        of pure juice—divides them.

2.

Luella, saying she'd like to treat me
    to a run-through of the whole
lime churn cycle, grasps
    six fat limes
delved from a deep fruit basket (delivered
brimful
    by farm picker this morning),
      whacks each lime
into near equal clean halves
with a single flick

      of her cutlass. A magic trick, of sorts,
        she tosses the limes in the air
          so quickly—one by one—
            her swung blade
    chops the fruit in two, while she snatches

                    both halves
        with one hand, sends each next
                    lime spinning
            overhead with the other — no time
                    lapsed between moves,

or so it appears. She clamps the machete
    betwixt all-but-toothless gums,
in those brief intervals
    after each lime
slashing . . . *Youse quite de juggler,* Thomas
baits her.
        *Close down de factory, and give
        show bizness*
a tumble. Unfazed by Thom's
flattery, she drops

        the dozen lime halves in *de Mishmosh Tub,*
            and twists the crank with muscly
                shoulder heft, whereby sharp
                    roller blades
        gnash and chomp limes with toothy sprockets,
                            expelling
            thick spurts of juice and pulp
                    into a bucket
                placed below the outlet tube
                    to catch the slushy

runoff. Then she peels the clean-scraped
    flat lime skins from the deep tub
interior with her long-
    handled tongs,
drops them in the trashbin. She now gathers
lime seeds
    with her flat scoop, tosses them
        in a bird feeder
hooked to the utility pole
outside her window.

        At last, she empties the bucket of mixed
            juice, rind bits and lumpy pulp
                    into a barrel, drains off

       all pure juice
through a wide hose attached in mid-stanchion,
        then transfers
  the drained sediments to a castiron
      squat boiler tank
      and lights the flamy gas jet
        below the base. . . .

3.

     Soon, a low hiss
    and sizzle grows to sputter—a crackling
  like wind-swept brush fire.
     The dense sediment potage
  in the tank heats
from slow simmer to full boil, the whole lumpy broth
    fuming up into cloudy vapors,
a thick greenish smoke which billows along the wide
vent pipe atop the tank,
    next passing through a long spiral coil, where
   the mixed gases cool and condense,
then trickle, slowly,

        into an open pot
on the floor. Our Luella pours the vessel's
       contents through a filter
     wide at the top but narrow
         as a pinprick
beneath, which rapidly leaks out the water, and thereby
      separates oil from thin H_2O,
heavy lime oil a pure distillate which she collects
        in recycled rum bottles—
  the old brand labels steamed or scraped off.
    These small jugs, sealed with candle
        wax or corks, she sells

   directly to local
  manufacturers of lime candies, aftershave,
  or other male toiletries—
   though a high percentage

       of her stock's
        saved for export, mostly to Great Britain or Canada.
          At our first pause for breath
    (her talk of specs, temps, formulas, near constant
    before now), I point
          to mammoth barrels near the opposite wall:
        How do those jumbo casks fit in?,
I ask. *Dem biggest tanks*

                    are for de bay oils,
        she replies. *Big crinkly bay leaves needs*
               de most space. Thereupon,
        she dumps three tall basketfuls
               of wide bay leaves —
loosely jumbled together — into the tallest giant vat
            standing on tiptoe to reach
      over the rim; then, turning up the gas jet's fire
              to the limit, she raises
    the temp beneath the rude castiron boiler
        stationed beside the vat. And soon,
                  the liquid within, hotly

      aboil, is bubbling
    and spitting gases like a witch's cauldron.
She twists the spigot counter-
    clockwise, opening all the valves:
much superheated
steam discharged fiercely into the bin, and we hear
    those bay leaves go roiling
and churning round and round, repeated steam blasts
scorching the turgid leaves
    until all their swelled fluids and serums
    burst the leaf skins, threads, stems —
the great leaf whirlpool

                emitting vapors
    intensely fragrant. Before long, we catch
          whiffs of strong bay aromas
        leaking from those tiny cracks
            along barrel seams,
and a wonderful scent it is! . . . We three chat, idly,

                    for perhaps a full quarter hour,
          while fresh spurts of piping hot steam are funneled
                              into the shuddering leaf bin
          at two or three minute restless intervals,
                    until such time as Luella's assured
                                        that every fat ripe leaf

               has been wrung dry
          of its fumy elixirs. Whenever she pumps
               steam fury into the full vat,
                    quick blasts of mist and spray
          fly out the bottom
          vent pipe — she collects these squirts of condensed
               bay mixture in a wide low pan,
     two fluid layers clearly separate, the one afloat
     above the other. No skillful
               filtering needed in this case, she neatly
               tilts the pan at a certain angle
     and that precious layer

                         of bay oil slides off
               the underlying water in a single patch:
                         the oil shines out, flaringly,
                         like sheets of aluminum foil.
                                        Pure bay extract,
          too, she siphons into old bottles corked for sale,
                    mostly to the bay rum factory
               across the road, or to chem labs, where bay oils
                              are refined for prompt use
                    in the manufacture of a colorful range
                         of medicines and drugs. Just now,
                                   she delights to give me

               the full rundown
                    and inventory of valued salves, curatives
          or little-guessed byproducts
                    sprung from her twin artistries:
          lime oils, bay oils
               distilled in tandem. Luella, my jill of all trades,
                    chanting a hymn to her labors,
     waves one arm to the East, seaward: *juiciest lime*

groves be thereabouts; then waves
 her other arm backwards to the Northwest
 and foothills below Chance's Peak:
best largeleaf bay tree

 farms thataways!
She swings both arms together, her hands
 pointed inward to her breasts:
 "Here! It all come together here,
 in my many times
uptorn and rebuilt plantation manor house. Always,
 I be gettin' de best bay leaves,
 de prime grown limes, since limeys and baypickers
 all be my best chums. De pickers
 be lookin' out for me, find me best fruits
 in their crop harvest, best leafage,
 twice per year. And I, too,

 looks out for them;
 I push'n squeeze their tightfisted bosses
 to pay them de better wage,
 to give them gentler work hours,
 de better pensions
 and health benefits. I won top business and quality
 production awards, four years
without fail, not to feather me own feeble sixty-
year-old's drab nest, believe me,
 nor to spice up me own fry chickie wings,
 but to lend a hand to all me friends,
sweet planters and pickers

 in farms and groves.
 We all be in it together — don't think we
 forget de next one needs us.
 Always, I be there for them,
 they there for me,
 and dat's it! You ask, did I start something new
 here, some enterprise nobody
 ever concocted before me, this four years? Well,
 no and yes. No, lots of folks
 be distilling oils from de crushed limes,

                many fewer boils up de bay leaves
                    for duh rich ooze of vapors

        and oils dat well up
           from de very strings and skins of leaf,
    widest choice full-bodied
        leaves you ever saw in de land.
But yes, I be first
    to combine these two flourishing local industries
        in one compact house factory:
two local crops dat give our tiny land much fame
abroad, de double source
    of our nation's pride be here first joined
        in my sole one-woman boilerworks.
O.K. You wormed my deeproot

                secrets outta me,
      but I'se too proud to be holdin' back
           my blessed livelihood tricks
    of de trade from likes of you.
                  You'll write de truth,
Thomas says. And spread word of our island's gifts
            and beauties to de across-seas
worlds . . ." So saying, she flips open a low hidden
                trapdoor in the bay leaf hotbox,
            catches the vast mass of steam-blasted
                dried leaves in her ballooning
                    thin plastic sacks, akin

      to our Glad Bags
        (godsend catchall at fall leafraking time),
ties up two of these cloud-
        blowzy inflated sacks with twine,
and hurls both bags
    into the squarish furnace that greeted our arrival
        with thick gush of smoke. . . . And now,
she sparkles the leaf pile with her pocket torch —
then waves us the joyous hails
    of goodbye, a swirly maelstrom of billows
        framing her stocky wholeearthblaze
silhouette of person.

WIND-SURFER'S REVENGE AT HORSESHOE BATTERY

(Fort Berkeley, Antigua)

... at Fort Berkeley, still stands one of the two posts for the chain that was hung across English Harbour to keep unwanted ships out. The other end of that chain was strung from what was called Horseshoe Battery, part of Fort Charlotte, which is no longer standing. ...

1.

Pigeon's Point
    Beach (the next bay South
        of our shore perch, across English Harbour
    and beyond this rocky nub
of land)—that's the place to swim
    and snorkel. But not here! These offshore shallows,
        so soupy thick with ship discharge,
            are putrid, scummy,
                a chemical mix of old fuels, lye-
                    acid detergents
                and hull rust scrapings from the harborage
        slipway repairs. ... Three local boys
            emerge: two slim

bikinied
    teenagers, one naked
        potbellied ten-year-old: diving by that antique
    beached barge, skins so mucky
and befouled with poisons (both lead
    and mercury abound), who can tell which swimmer
        is scantily clad, which suitless,
            bareassed? If we preach
                to *them* the hazards of mercury
                    poisoning (two days
                abed with high fevers, swollen limbs, swelled
            tongue—then, death or snap revival),
                or carcinogens'

lethal buildup,
    they'd snicker and scoff.
        All the same, I propose you recite your smack
        safety spiel — then I may get
my headstart up the weedchoked dirt path
    to Fort Berkeley, a pair of turreted segments
        of stone wall which visibly flank
            bends in the cliff rim
                overhead (I need a big leadoff
                    to try to match
                your uphill pace, son). . . . Now I hear your voiced
            genial lessons — more pep talk
                than wrangle —

muffled by lap
    of shore waves below
        as I ascend, the boys' playful cries squeaked
    above your manly late-teen frog
croakings, their high pitch heightened
    by shrill echoes perhaps. *So soon you're beside me!*
        Now a distance ahead, then above,
            in so few seconds —
                you unhurried and barefoot, while I,
                    puffing to keep up,
                        stumble, though my sneakers afford some traction
                    and protection from thorns, glass,
                        or stinging ants

(your bare soles
    immune to such?); stalled,
        breathless, I catch glints of your leica lens
    lifted over your head, shoulder
strap still visible under your armpit.
    You swerve from side to side, pursuing a mobile
        subject, the whole shaved cliff scarp
            no more than a few
                meters wide, but you give chase, looping
                    and cutting back:
                        so absorbed in the game pursued, it's a wonder
                        you don't plunge down the steep abyss
                            into cove, inlet.

≈ 56

Do your feet
    touch earth, or ride air
        cushions? Where do you find toe hold for swerves
    and leaps, broad jumps in tight
close quarters? . . . At last, I do catch up.
    You're a shrewd hunter, fleet of foot and agile
        in pursuit, but your deft quarry —
            four scrawny goats
                (rib cages engraving stark outlines
                    on bloated abdomens) —
                outfox you every time: rapscallions, not models!
        When you think you have two goats trapped
            in ideal poses

on your film's
    optic screen (balanced, say,
        upon that flat-topped battlement of fort wall),
    they dodge askew, eluding your slow
trigger finger. The shutter jumps, ever,
    a fraction of a second too late — the lens eye's
        aperture flashing on vacancy —
            each exposed frame
                stunned blind, wiry subjects fled,
                    escaped. The goats do
            a slapstick dance. Little Chaplinesque backskips.
    Surprise upward leaps. Side-hops.
        Airborne spins.

Do they tease
    the gullible camera
        marksman? At times, they seem to pose and wait,
to assist your well-aimed shots;
but whenever you get them in focus,
    unblurred, well-lit, they spring awry. Two or three
        seem to pace each other, to dance
            in formation
                like stunt pilots or figure skaters,
                    only to break ranks
                at the last possible instant, flying off
            in oblique trajectories, or arcs,
                whereby they cheat

lens's capture
   of all but a rear hoof,
      half a foreleg, or a bobbing tail and butt
   section truncated in the frame's
upper corner; or perhaps, a halved
   goat face in profile, Picassoesque, pointy chin
      trailing its wisp of beard —
         but no ear, nor
            upper jaw or snout. Even so, you won't
               give up the chase!
            On bended knee one moment. Astride wall top
         the next. . . . *I leave you to perfect*
            cliff pirouettes.

2.

               Unearthly yowls,
         arisen from the rough whitecapped sea
   surface below — whether of joy
      or agony? — pierce my trance.
Indistinguishable,
   at first, from the roar of surf exploding into rocky
      breakwater, the shrieks — timed
   at uncertain intervals — outrival, at last, all
competing zings, pops,
      rumbles . . . I hasten to the crag's far edge,
         lean over the rim, and peer
below, sighting down
                  the steep escarpment
   of shore rock, hunting the source.
      The promontory's upper third, or so, was carved
and moulded by thousands
   of slave laborers who hacked the fort battlements
      with primitive axes, sledge
         hammers, from bare rock: most man-honed buttresses fallen
   into crumbled heaps,
      today. But the few wall segments
   left intact reveal the whole outline
         of dismantled fort's original turreted
            roof. The lower

two thirds of cliff base, polished
and buffed to a high sheen
by the millenniums of pounding whitecaps,
is blindingly aglow, in spots —
the glare so pungent
I must look

away, then back,
by fits and starts. Or I find I can steady
my gaze by shifting my purview
to one outermost stone flank,
or to another —
but never meeting the gleamy rock face point blank. Now,
slowly tracking few last echoes
of that strident voice, my eyes rove from surf-foamy
cliff shoreline seawards.
And I must fight sieges of vertigo, dizziness
triggered by the precipitous
dropoff, a sheer plunge
to coast-reef coral,
six inches — less than a halfstep! —
in front of my toes. *Woozy, woozy,* I backstep.
Peer out from cliff margin.
Pivot neck slowly: moves dreamlike, I circle
the horizon, my sight lines
shimmering like lighthouse beams. At last, I connect
with one lone white sail
gliding shoreward, a black stalwart
figure astride the single angled mast,
his Olympian carriage and ripply physique
a sapling braced

parallel to leaning-forward
canvas, his stark outline
bikini-clad, silhouetted against the sail's
white backdrop, bare feet propped —
unshakably — on wafer
thin flake

of board. He approaches,
at breakneck rip, the base of my lookout.

I can see his toes curl, glued
            to the slick plank skimming
        the surface — airborne,
    for moments, his vessel skips from swell to humped swell,
            while I circle jagged Cape
    border, monitoring my compass point's projection:
longitude and latitude
        gauged for playful convergence with wind surfer's
            beeline to shore ... *May he see me*
wave — standing on tiptoe —
                        my tall greetings!
        Suddenly, he unlooses a volley
    of fierce groans, the renewed outpouring signalled
by his widemouthed grimace
one prolonged moment before the great wails, delayed
        by sea distance between us,
    can reach my ears. Those disembodied chants seem to issue
from a source far behind
            his dashing one-winged hydroplane,
    that hurled projectile of himself
            looming over the horizon like a Kamikaze
                human torpedo

            aimed at my vulnerable roost.
    I shudder, fearing a Triton's
        power to pulverize to smithereens whole cliff
            scarp: bulwark to my squat fiftyish
                balding and pudgy frame,
                    squirrely

            in broad-brimmed straw
        sun hat and tattered levis' cutoffs; I to be
snuffed out — frail babybird exploded
        from its nest — when that stone floor
beneath my feet shatters!
I know it shall disintegrate entire, like a crystal vase,
        when the wave frequency vibes
of our wind surfer's hollers reach a pitch to burst
walls of solid rock;
        or the manned rocket of his craft rams the crag's
            foundations, whichever strikes first.
So I flee that center

                    of impact, myself alone
         the torpedo's target, and I pass
      each successive gap in the survived wall segments,
sighting the self-hurtled
wave rider through each topless turret window,
         in turn, thinking: *each slot
         held cannon in time past   each fit casing to house cannon
         still*   And I reach, at last,
         the one noble artillery relic
that survives intact — colossal
         bronze cannon, mounted in its window casement
            at the curved loop

         of the fort's far end; its barrel
      is levelled, directly,
         at the arrowing human projectile undeflected
            from his suicide course. Now I lift
               and lower the great wide-
               throated gun shaft,

         tremblingly, and I take
            sure aim, making ready to light short fuse
with my pocket torch. The brave rider
         of the single puff-bellied white wing
      yelps and wails and croons,
         as never before, while he bucks and opposes the choppiest
            waves below; grappling, as well,
the gustiest winds in his teeth, knifing that air wall,
demoniac, into shore.
      If his faraway whoops had carried amazing distance
         to my cliff-high ears, his revived
howls strike pained eardrums
                     bitingly raw and close
         as if my common ear cups have grown
            wide-lipped as queen conch shells, and the demon blows
keen bellows of his voice
directly into each shell chamber. Ah! His shrieks
         match those of hawks and gulls
      riding the strong gale currents overhead, one-winged cousin
      to the lovely raptors, he,
            human mast and sail hawk, so wild and free
      he's both wing and winged seed sprung

newbirthed from its pod. And have I, spellblinded,
    fired red-hot cannonball

flaming into his breast, just prior
to his most certain impact
    with the shore wall propping my cowardly stance,
        my hunched shoulders pitched backwards
            as the cannon recoils . . .
        But he's saved,

    who drops the rope sheet
        letting the taut sail go slack and flutter;
    while he backflips, his midriff arched
        in a perfect reverse dive, head thrown
    back, his two hands cupped
together spear-pointing his plunge, heels over head, ducked
    quick: the whole blade shaft of streamlined
flesh convulsed, but once, and vanished below the sea face;
his descent the frictionless
    pure streak of a hawk spearing mackerel, himself
        first kin to the osprey, evermore.
His body flashed, one time —
                he's gone, long and long
    below, *whence and whither to emerge?* . . .
    Not soon. Not near, mumbles the softer-voiced swells
barrel-rolling into shore.
The tipped sailcraft, once fallen, flops and bobs,
    aimless, like a long-dead fish
carcass, pale belly upwards floating, white jetsam of flesh
    gone putrid . . . The wind surfer's
        cries, still echoing in my ears, bespeak
    ages past. The many ranks of British
        gunboats, hid in these dockyards, were battle-
            launched from this harbor

        of a hundred years of seesawing
    rivalries, power struggles
        with French fleets, Spanish galleons, Dutch;
            even commissary patrols from pirate
                outposts based in nearby
                islet chains

≈ 62

                    given heartiest chase
            by the warships ensconced in this deep-bottomed
    harborage. Do I not hear, today, ghost
            tongues of the many past ship captains,
    those halest ship crews,
        sigh again, who would cheer and salute history's ten thousand
            daybreaks anew, in echoes of our wind-surf
    jockey's bronco-buster Carib howls and yodeled love cries?
    The many warring factions
        come back, come back, their far voices rekindled
            in your hawk-ravenous bursts of song,
O *solitary one-sail winger*
                        of these lonely-waved harbor
        shores, your one voice begotten from afar,
            redoubled, and passed into time future . . . Collapsed
    sailboard, pitched to and fro
on small wave crests, drifts back into deeper waters,
            lolling away from shore; suddenly,
    in the middle distance, the short mast pops upright, poised
    beside an erect blackgold
            shining figure resurrected from the harbor
    deeps, who takes up afresh the cord end
            of his sheet, spreading wide, as before, his ghost
                white sail-wing of a hawk!

3.

I'm stirred from dream
    lull, a hiatus, by goat squeaks—
        revived sounds of the chase, hunt and scuffle,
    those teenager mock-soprano
trills and warbles blent with Isaac's
    gruff throaty *whoas* and *gotchas*. . . . That trio of dockyard
            muck-swimmers, creole dryads, have scaled
                steep cliffsides
                    in two minutes flat, blazing a shortcut
                        from the spillway wharf
                    and pier below, shrinking, by furlongs, uphill hike
                I'd laboriously trudged, on prescribed paths,
                    hours back. And Isaac

pursues the fugitive
    goats, still — switching lenses,
        reciting oaths and humming chants of the hunt
    to bewitch the barnyard escapees
into submission. The boys, keeping in step
    with the goats, mix and mingle so dexterously, all
        seven creatures — weaving in and out
            of camera's wideangled
                prospect — become undifferentiable
                    in the swift flux
                    and jumble of chase, while Isaac guns them down,
                his film shots a foil to my cannon blasts
                    at the lone surfer.

The nude small boy,
    snatching one goat upwards
        in his arms, hugs the creature to his bare chest
    kicking and mewling (the goat, wider
than the child is long, projects thin snout
    to one side, hind legs and wriggly tail to the other) —
        Now shoot us, he begs, the other boys
            posing behind him,
                no fellow goats left anyplace in sight,
                    absconded in distance
                until day's end, truant hoofed models, at best . . .
            Soon, a whole roll of our film's cranked
                to the blank dead

end of the strip,
    no shots left; the last frame,
        like the final cannonball, signs off this day's
    multiple adjacent cliff-top rounds
of artillery practice. But each model, happily,
    has taken at least one turn clutching the trapped Billy,
        Isaac and I, likewise, embracing
            the unlucky captive —
                who never stops squirming, and, vengeful
                    at the last, awards *me*,
                only, his fragrant signature, in two well-aimed
                    splatters evenly dappling my neck, shirt
                        pockets and collar.

≈ 64

4.

        Now and again, absently,
           in the midst of camera romps, I find I catch
careless views of the solo sail artist
        riding and curvetting the wind gusts,
speedily, into the cove;
        or recovering his fallen crumpled fleece of white, adrift,
           bobbed out to the harbor mouth,
then snapping the mast upright in a sudden heroic twist,
steadied and balanced
        beside his angled black protean carriage.
        But now I feel, subliminally,
a void in the luminous bay,
                before my practiced
        surveyor eye notes the sail's abrupt
        disappearance from any remote corner of the surf-
jockey's whitecapped turf
and racer's arena. I run to the near cliff edge
        vista — no sail parked on shore
        or wedged between rocks; *has he been sucked under?* I question
the wave ripples, wordlessly,
           when I hear a deep-throated baritone
voice halfway between the Jamaican
        actor whose natural rubato hymns the UNCOLA
           SEVEN-UP ads on TV

        and steel drum's rumbled timbre:
that rapid-fire volley
        of twinned BOOM BOOMs aimed directly at my person!
           I fall to my knees, then duck my head
              before I meet, again,
           wave skimmer's

        blazing eyes at close range,
           who squats like a horseman on the dolphin-gray
humped back of our one cannon, removed
        from its wall socket and spun around,
pointing its barrel snout
at my breastbone, me sprawled and clutching (of all useless
        defenses) my comic throat, aghast . . .
The second cannoneer, surmounting the cliff slopes

   in still fewer seconds
     than the children's recent hillside dash, winks
    at my prostrate figure—his conquest,
saying, with his eyes only:
        I saw you fire cannonball
   down upon my innocent light craft,
    and now I return my fire, perhaps evening the score.
He dismounts, swivelling
  the huge castiron barrel a full one-hundred-eighty
     degrees on its circular wheel base,
   repositioned in the turret niche. Next, he leads our passel
  to the very tall post
    stationed at the cliff rim farthest
  from the cannon, takes a gymnast's
    grip of the last link-hoop of chain fragment
     fastened to the pole's top,

   and swings up and down, those arcs
  widening with each rise
    and fall of his legs until, finally, his peak
     undulation sends him above the post,
      his legs pointed skyward:
     a pole vaulter

   at the vertex of his jump.
    And indeed, his profile is close mirror image
to the sleek backwards dive he executed
   a while back from the unsteady platform
of toppling sailcraft—
that performance cheered, in solitude, by a secret audience
    of one, myself. . . . Now he settles
on bare feet beside his historic maypole, which we can see,
as he holds forth,
   is true summit of the island's northeast corner—
   though surpassed, of course, by his winged
legs! He points to a cliff arm,
         near match for the high ridge
  we occupy now, on the peninsular loop
   of land, ashimmer, just opposite English Harbour
from us: "A second post, mate
to this one, stood just so, on Horseshoe Battery";
   the latter, fallen into disrepair

    many years back, collapsed and plummeted from the cliff ledge
   when young Robespierre
      was a small child. Prime chunks of the core
of that historic timber, he elaborates,
     were carved by his older brothers into wind-surfer
       boards and masts. And he rides,

    today, a torpedolike sail-propelled
   plank salvaged from the wreck
     of one such prized board, bequeathed by his brother
       (wrapped in its shroud of gashed canvas),
        lain idle for seven years
     of his puberty;

    until he'd taught himself
     minimal shipbuilder and carpentry arts needed
to refurbish the jagged-edged, splintered,
    and sea-begrimed slab (but not cracked
or warped, the central grain
of the old tree marvelously intact, impervious, it seemed,
    to Time's or the Sea's wear); whittled,
sanded and polished, slightly shrunken, but dimensions
honed to exact scale
    of the progenitor, without loss of the board life's
    innate spring, if a tad more streamlined,
he boasts — his eyes aglow,
         as if he's been praising
   human ally, or sentient comrade akin
   to himself and moulded, somehow, in his own self-
image. *His board*, alone,
carries the embossed sovereign seal and engraved
     stamp of the seventeenth-century
    late Governor of the Leeward Islands Council who, singly,
persuaded the British Crown
    by a flurry of letters, two years running,
to adopt this very harbor — matchless
     for its cavernous breadth and unplumbed deeps —
      as the West Indies home

    for her Majesty's Royal Fleet . . .
   He offers to escort us
     below, for a view of the revered heirloom — parked

and hidden in his secret cove, our troop
                to have a firsthand peek
                        at the august

            Governor's hand-scripted royal
                Imprimatur. But glad believers of the first order
    he finds us all, not a sceptic among us,
            not even the goat — becalmed at long last
    in Isaac's gentled clasp
            (who else's light and caressive touch might tame wild goat?);
                waiting out his discourse, we greet
his first real pause with our question: "Why two identical
towering posts, each rooted
        in rocky cliffs, on opposite sides of famed harbor,
        a distance of perhaps a full half mile
yawning between them?" Cheerily,
                            he takes up the loose thread,
            spinning a tale of two posts, both hewn
        from a single great Carib oak trunk: one erected
at either harbor mouth
    extremity of the horseshoe, which he traces, now,
            with the sweep of his right arm
        and the graceful wave of his finger wand: one here at Fort
Berkeley (we now congregated
            around that *survivor*), the other stationed
at Fort Charlotte — the battlement walls
            crumbled and ground to gravel, or less; some pieces
                of fortress recognizable, still,

        across the bay, but most stone columns
    or fallen wall units seem blent —
            to our eyes — with shore rocks. The absentee post,
                uprooted by two centuries of storms
                    and toppled into the sea,
                            was salvaged,

        in stray driftwood chunks,
            by his brothers; while this post, Fort Berkeley's
most salient landmark, was preserved (stained
            with primitive varnishes, shellacs), kept up
    by five generations
        of governors for historic charm — its placement beside dockyards

        and other memorial outposts the key
to its survival, down to these scattered fragments of fort wall
nodding, comically,
      from disjoined patches of cliff rim; some few blocks
      leaning seaward, others all-but-tumbled
back upon cliff interior . . .
                    So saying, he lifts the end loop
    of broken-off chain hung from the tower,
      this residual segment a mere scrap of the mile-long
original which spanned
the full width of harbor mouth twice, anchored to tops
      and midsections of those twin poles;
    no one link of either stout cable bent, corroded, or severed
in three decades of skirmishes
        launched by the English fleet from this one port —
the damaged ships returned, always,
        to Nelson's Dockyard and Spillway for speedy repairs,
          premiere boatworks of these seas.

5.

In my palm he drops
    that wrist-thick iron relic,
      last link of the surviving dangled fragment
of colossal double chain that hung
between towers, and I'm amazed at its weight:
    three times a normal horseshoe's thickness, six times
        its mass and bulk. I inspect the links,
          eight in all, shocked
              that we hadn't noticed their magnitude
                when Robespierre swung
            acrobatically from the chain, his feat applauded
by the kids long after. So struck were we
        by his pendulum

climb to the post's
    upper limits and beyond,
      the chain links' uncommon dimensions escaped
    our notice . . . Ruminant, I hazard
my next question: why had the first harbor
    masters undertaken — at great expense — the labor to forge

and galvanize (multiple zinc coatings,
      sea-acid-resistant)
           the Carib World's sturdiest and longest
                consecutive-linked
           sweep of chain. To which he gives, ivories aglint,
      his broadest smile: "They slaved to fence out
           all enemy ships!"

No Spanish caravels
    or triplemasted French
         high-speed frigates powerful enough to burst
    this chain's weakest link. Imagine it!
No single metallic ringed ZERO, not one forged-
    iron cipher, among some five thousand ten-inch-diameter
         links (per each drooped single expanse
              of chain), ever cracked:
                   a total ten thousand loops, winners all!
                        The chains, he fancies,
                   were live organisms in themselves, each sensitive
              to variables of temperature, wind gusts,
                   or humidity. Hour

by hour, each chain
    grew more taut or more slack,
         lifting or lowering a few meters in a day;
    the individual links so resilient,
so supple, they afforded a maximum range
    of gradations to the serpentine twisted spans afloat
         between towers. One expanse was known
              to droop or straighten
                   far more than the other, owing, partly,
                        to modest divergence
                   in altitude, or distances from sea level: chain slump
              ratios accruing from the sum total of unique
                   independent link-

body metabolisms,
    stress resistance factors
         related to the mysterious giant aircrafts'
    metal fatigues of our own day—
still much unknown about safe longevities

in diverse weathers, at early and advanced ages: metals
    age, enduring or mouldering at their own
        sweet eccentric pace,
            like the humans who hand-battered them alive
                and left their own souls'
                    stain imbued in each chain link. Prompted by our host,
    then, we marvel at the high reliability index
        of so many thousands

of iron *cheerios*,
    not one link flawed enough
        to fracture in collisions with those heavy-
hulled warboats of the conquistador
Spanish Armada. Only twice, in thickest pall
    of night mists (so proclaims the harbor logs, kept daily,
        in those war-frenzied years), did fleets
            of invader ships
                attempt a surprise assault on English Harbour —
                    but no vessel's charge
                could burst those chains. One grim page of ship's ledger,
            however, reports one-hundred-yard-deep gashes
                hacked into a frigate's

bow, above and below,
    by a *phantom aerial buzzsaw*.
        First mate's eyewitness oath and deposition:
"Ship's hull take de slash as coconut
rind catch shucks from dem pickers' machetes."
    None saw the secret weapon, night fog so thick, but many
        were given to speculate upon the powers
            of witchcraft unleashed
                upon their vessels — as seamen are prone to do
                    when faced with unearthly
                      omens, who know the fogged sea may hatch dark specters.
            They beheld their great ships mauled, run afoul,
                though not one cannonball

or pistol shot was fired.
    Two invasion attempts, both
        quashed by those airborne knives madly whirled
    at the bows, severing sails and masts

        like so many swiftly amputated limbs — all fleets
           of the enemy were forewarned, thereby, to confine attacks
              on British ships to open seas. . . . I grasp,
                  in both hands, that one
                      terminal chain link (*metal donut, iron bagel*) —
                        but cannot bring myself
                          to touch my tongue to the curved ring's coolness; so I lay
                    my cheek against the gorge in that magic loop
                  and shut my eyes,

letting the fogbound
        mishmash of desperate sailor
            hands, crushed yardarms, severed masts, torn sails,
        sheets and riggings start to tremble anew:
whether the thrilled vibes be my own mere blood thump
        palpitant against the ZERO round single handcuff pressed hard
            into my face veins and neck's jugular, plugging,
                thus, the fifty-year-old's
                    already blunted circulation; or if it be stored-up
                      ineradicable memory
                  of metal revived in the atoms, transmitting its magnetic
        energy field into my mind's receptor template . . .
                And I brush three bottom

links across my forehead,
        one by one, then hear great howls
            of the stunned and bewildered forward watch boatswain
            catapulted, oddly, from his lookout roost
by invisible fog-hid rings interlocked, snapping the post
        supporting his canopied seat like a dried twig, while he struggles
            to translate the messages of his senses, quizzically,
                into the echo chamber
                    of his megaphone (built-in bullhorn and loudspeaker),
                      and warn his fellow
                        sailors of the cataclysm befalling the ship, even as he flies
                headlong over the riven and shattered bow
            into the blind dumb sea. . . .

2 ≈ Earlier Poems

ORANGE COUNTY PLAGUE: SCENES

SCENE 1: Dislocations

In Orange, tree-plague has struck the mile-long groves. Greased
Chainsaws slide through trunks as knives slice butter.
Autos skid in the orangesap treejuice
Blend flooding the gutter.
Psychotic farmers hallucinate glues
To restore limbs slashed by sharktoothed steeljawed beasts.
If some of the screws are loose,
It doesn't matter.
At least,
Teenage lovers scatter
Back to the parks. They cruise
From bench to bench, and a few coolcats grow chaste
Perhaps. There is less temptation to bruise
Forbidden fruit – a daughter
Waits for her father's permission to choose
Her life. Blood-mistakes are small enough to blotter,
Like smudges of ink. Loss-of-faith is mended with library paste.

SCENE 2: Stump Fugue

In unison, hundreds of shovels vanish under stumps. They descend
By regular strokes, like oil-drills. Workmen's faces
Whiten; their bodies absent, statuesque.
White knuckles, weightless,
Glitter in the failing sun. Dusk
Attends the snapping of roots. Arms, self-moving, blend
With saws. The sun's disc
In the last oasis
Sinks. *Send*
Rain where the Human Race is
Still tree-loving, still able to risk
Life to preserve the beauty that lives. What sickens, mend!
Great fists of roots in trucks whisk
Up Coast Hi-way, menacing crisis:

WIDE LOAD marked in red. The clay-stuck
Upturned stumps, tree-corpses, bounce on the chassis
And sway . . . clotted hands, upcast, clutching madly at the wind.

SCENE 3: Freeway Skeletons

(a deserted grove: mostly dead trees, rotten fruit)

Near the freeway, the unburied dead raise delicate skeletons, brittle
Arms extending frail hands — mock-perch for birds.
In a light breeze the air is black
With falling fingers; words
From the dying lips of lynchees, their luck
Run out — the crackle of twigs; last drools of spittle —
Drops of sap that fleck
The bark, wood's
Blood. *Ill
Winds rattle old boards
(Or bones) in America's (hush!) rack-
Negroes slaughterhouse*. The passing motorists, cattle
Armed to butcher each other, slack
Their speed to loot. Rewards
Are few. But the thieves have a special knack
For sorting the stray good orange from the rotting hoards.
Listen for the moos. Chewing of the cud. The spirit's death-rattle.

SCENE 4: Tree Burning

At the center of a stump-studded field, a disordered pyre, strewn
With mangled tree-carcass, waits. Branches, at all
Angles, prevent neat piling of logs.
An indignity too subtle
For the influx of watchers (pyros) begs
Notice. For hours, blood-thirst in the air has grown.
Eyes, unwinking, glare. Legs
Stiffen into metal.
Night. No moon.
Lit match! Odd chanting. A riddle.
Burn, witch, burn! Crochety old bags

Burn. Witch, burn, witch! Nigger-witch. Which nigger? One!
How spot a witch? Check for wigs,
Or black mustache. Telltale
Itch in the crotch, sticky lips: Nigger-stags!
Or check bold strut, briar tongue, fire in the eyes, mettle.
Guilt stinks under the arms and dons old rags. Nigger-witch, burn!

SCENE 5: Preservatives

Mid-day. A mammoth Redwood creeps on wheels. Four lanes of autos,
Reluctant, bestow reverence; the giant's funeral
Hearse shambles. The corpse, exposed,
Has not begun to smell.
Tree-flesh, unembalmed, won't rust
Or rot. Tree bodies outlast tree souls. Mulattos,
In America's death-in-life lust
Agony, grow beautiful
As trees. Bistros
Are mills where blackwhite people
Logs are cut to prayer size; kiss-Christ
Blues — a holy rage of buzzsaw jazz . . . *sham Castros*
Preach re-growth from severed roots . . .
Boogie-and-twist swivel
Hips roll — tree limbs in tornados tossed.
Battered Races, timbers that seem to rise as they fall,
Murderously blossom in the suffering and dancing country of ghettos.

SCENE 6: The American Halfway

Above, the farm and pasture — halfway — the metropolis below,
Smog in the eyes and throat, dung-stink in the nose,
Fordtruck in the front yard, moocow in back;
That's how you sing the halfway blues.
On the freeway, herded twelve-deep in dumptrucks,
Stooped on the warped floorboards of stalls (Jim Crow
In the Deep South, spics
Out West) braceros
Sing. Sow
Beanfields gold in the sunrise,

    Half-frozen all night in pasteboard shacks!
    Free country good for beez-ness. Amor in Meh-hee-koh.
    (Slave labor don't mind the dirt wages: Mex
    Eat crow.) They file through bean-rows,
    Swift and frail as antelope. If anyone ask,
    Why drudge all day in sun-fire, strings for clothes?
    Ah-meh-ree-kuh ees work! eat! sleep! Amor in Meh-hee-koh!

SCENE 7: The Wire Forests

    On their sides, resembling fallen timbers without rough
    Barks — a hundred feet apart — lie power poles.
    Just yesterday, this road was edged
    With Eucalyptus; in aisles
    Between rows of trees, seats for the aged.
    Now tree-odors hover in the air, residues of life.
    The poles are erected. The frigid
    Passionless verticals
    Strive
    To fill the socket-shaped holes
    Left by trees. Identical, cement-wedged
    Below, parasitically fastened to live wires above —
    Tree-impostors, never to be budged
    From a telegraphic owl's
    Knowitallness, they stand — rigid!
    Sad children, wishing to climb, scan the miles
    And miles of uninterrupted electric forests for leaves.

SCENE 8: Tree Praise

    Beauty is poorness of posture, a studied unevenness of frame.
    Trees have sex appeal, gnarled character, a stubborn
    Knottiness: a refusal to grow one way;
    Preference for curves, fork-turns
    Over a sapling's uprightness; asymmetry
    Of branches, leaf-shapes askew, imbalance of color-scheme.
    The Eucalyptus, obsessed with nudity
    Or eager for sunburn,
    Sheds lame

Barks as snakes slough skins.
The leaning Birch, to hide its branchless purity
Of form, loves to dance in a blinding gale, and for shame
Of the drab whiteness of bark, for eternity
Would spring up and back — and burn
In the driving wind. I think of the sway-
Backed Oak, the lackadaisical Willow, the Juniper, Hawthorn —
And a preference for woods over human society, at last, I proclaim.

SCENE 9: The Sterilization

Hydra-trees survive the death of parts. Some trees
Dead at the top outlive bad weather, poisons.
Decapitation cures. My Pepper
Tree (a kind of treason?)
Has become a bush. Trees, like lepers,
Slough their rotten limbs. Gratuitous sprays,
"Weed-killers," infect the upper
Earth. Do those men
Who squeeze
Death spray suffer my vision?
They sterilize loam in fields. The deadly vapors
Spread to my backyard. Today, in the faintest breeze —
Like beautiful hanks of hair in the barber
Shop — fall dried stem-
Husks, brittle, bewildered to sever
From roots and lie in useless piles, my Bougain-
Villea withered to brown scrolls of leafage . . . No rose.

SCENE 10: The View from the Kitchen

Sides sheared off, the sand level on the bottom, this river-bed
Is dry. The parallel cyclone fences entice scores
Of children to enter; without risk, play
Is dull. Forbidden tours
Follow KEEP OUT signs as crime follows prey.
FLOOD CONTROL threats replace NO FISHING. The mud
Is moistened with sewage. Debris
And watercress lure

Vagrants, mutts,
Wildlife. An occasional horse
And horseman, cyclists, tractors pass by
Alongside the ditch. In my kitchen I watch, and the skid-
Row scum watch back. *What can we say
To each other? Who is worse
Off?* In Winter, the fantastic rains wash away
Tons of dirt from the banks. *Nothing is safe in my house.*
In Spring, I measure the narrowing margin of earth near my yard.

SCENE 11: The Waves

House-high waves envelop the pier with algae, brine,
Sea-scum. The roughest surf in years excites
Beach bums to risk their skins. Life
Guards, who lift weights
After hours, imbibe their fill of grief.
The deaths they swallow turn to cramps in the groin.
Nightfall. High tides knife
Trenches in cliff-sides,
Undermine
Foundations of lavish estates.
Many slide downhill. One topples off
Into the sea, somersaulting over stilts, a falling crane
Or heron. Beach houses on a low bluff
Wash away like orangecrates.
Nothing slakes the hunger of the thief-
Pacific. Maddened by the tedium of days, he mates
With womanish earth. Anything human is chaff of the grain.

SCENE 12: The Ice Phallus

Frozen halibut is fresher than today's catch. Vacuum-packed
Bass in freezers grow purer than life. Time stops.
Ice crystals' skill competes with veteran
Seamen's. Fish essence sleeps
In stiffened flesh. In our future, semen
Shall cease to flow. Ice-birth will mend slacked
Morals and eliminate sin –

Love snarls and rapes,
Sex-locked.
An idle fisherman drops
Bait from the pier. Fish, like women
Immune, resist his hook. His rod is cracked,
His reel jammed with backlash, the line
snagged on a rock. Surfers' lips
Arc mockeries below, the mouths green-
Blue, sea-numbed. The highest breaker snaps
Torso-whips. The brain's deepfreeze they love, wave-bucked.

SCENE 13: Afterlife of a War-jet

(at a children's park)

Fresh coats of paint disguise the emblems of war. Maggots
Restoring the flesh of dead wolves to life
In the elixir of gnashing jaws and gut:
Children swarming in the *safe*
Cockpit and fuselage of a killer-jet,
A surprise package of doom in the hands of bigots.
Stale blood and fresh snotspit
Mix in the mouth-strafe
Of play. Tots
On the wings rehearse tough
Battle lingo, or they regurgitate
Movie war poses: salute, the march, rigor mortis.
Both with and without honor they commit
War crimes, and forget. The chafe
Of rough surface on hands and face whets
The appetite for more. Morticians render grief
Therapy. Death-play opens *all* of the emotion spigots.

SCENE 14: Mines and Missiles

(Naval Munitions Station, Seal Beach)

In plain view from Coast Highway, thousands of steel balls,
Arranged neatly as cans on the grocer's shelf,
Lie dormant. In World War II, they guarded

The nation's bodies from Adolf
Hitler, Mussolini, Hirohito. In morbid
Idleness they rest, their monomaniacal death-wills,
By munitions-surgery, rendered
Sterile. *A stray calf*
Moos. Gulls
Swoop off the coast. The gulf
Between TNT and the Atom is underscored
By the Atlas ICBMs, the length of the battleships' hulls,
Maneuvering in highway traffic. Shrouded
With canvas, they exceed half
Of the road's six lanes in width. The livid
Faces of motorists sicken, as they mutter gruff
Curses at the traffic deadlock. Oblivious to mines *or* missiles.

SCENE 15: Meditation Upon the Power House

Most of the County's vital organs, exposed to all weathers
And the bomb of assassin, form the power house.
Vulnerable, it hums in the night,
Quivers with a queer pulse.
Visible for miles, it looms in the soot-
Dark fields of the coast — a meteoric glow — and gathers
The dark into arteries of light-
Alchemy. Small wills
Smother
In *One* — encompassing *Else* —
That engenders power as swiftly as thought
Flashes in the brain. In the Great Whole, parts wither
Into the truth. Daybreak. When Lot's
Wife looked back, the Gospels
Tell, she changed to a pillar of salt . . .
Such risk the listener takes when, in daylight, he mulls
Over the divinity of a dynamo that resembles a grain elevator.

SCENE 16: Spotlights

A pulsating three-hundred-sixty degree incandescent eye,
On the clubhouse roof, patrols my midnight walk.

The moon is a spotlight too. Lights
Guard and watch; they mock
My secret thoughts with telltale watts.
The sacred grasses glitter like a black-green sea.
This is no place for halfwits
Who treasure the dark.
Bats. I
Walk soft, but my shadow, a block
Long, jerks like hiccups in the epiglottis.
I hunt myself on the links, out-of-bounds, a bit loony.
I seek my moon's dark side. Light waits
In ambush, behind my back.
In love or art, the Beloved shuts
Her eyes and turns her face from glare of daybreak.
The beam of the watchman's flashlight squelches immortality.

SCENE 17: Interference

Tonight, strolling the hills overlooking the shore, I gasp
At the beauty of an electric storm. My radio's static
Muddles the up-to-the minute news.
Punctual as a nervous tic,
The sea-and-skyscape, palpitant, glows.
Will the lovely pulse of the universe ever collapse?
How much there is to lose.
We forget. The cynic
Traps us
In ourselves, like a hypodermic.
I welcome tonight's interference: snows
On the TV screen, dimmed lights, an occasional lapse
In telephone service. *Cut the wires. I refuse
To answer the door.* The clock
Misses a tick. More than the wind blows.
In precious night, we touch. I pray for the fantastic
Messages one can learn to receive when the heartbeat skips.

WHELK HUNTER IN THE STAGHORNS

I. Flying on the Surface

    Aloft on the unpunctured float
Of lungs and flipper-rubber,
      I thread the needlefish with my spear, a snorkeling
         Headhunter: the gar leading
           With pointed nose,
        Two interlocked

    Rows of teeth, saw-edged,
That can cut a brother
      In two — the decapitated head snapping blindly
         At whatever passes before it,
           Long after the severed
        Body has fallen

    Away: needlefish javelins
Streaking after fry,
      Targets themselves for swooping birds: one gar, struck
         By a gull divebomber — instantly
           Disemboweled —
        Dies, a still live

    Minnow in its mouth. My forehead,
Submerged, konks
      The feet of a snoozing pelican, listless, drooping
         Discarded knotty branches
           Near the raft
        Of his broad bottom,

    Shading eleven small squids
Back-jetting in an undulant
      Double-V formation: a sine wave motion, ribbon-
         Winding from end to end.
           I jab at the middle
        Link: it spurts

　　　　Three feet ahead of the chain,
But divides in two,
　　　　Splits—no, doubles!—leaving an inky-black pseudomorph
　　　　　　　In its place, impaled round
　　　　　　　　　My spearpoint, thinning
　　　　　　　To a smoke-ring. Near

　　　　Stumpy Point, where bay-mouth
Meets open sea,
　　　　Breakers converging from three sides at once, mixing
　　　　　　　And chopping their flows, reinforcing
　　　　　　　　　Or cancelling by turns—
　　　　　　　I slip in shallow

　　　　Water, yellowtail on my spear.
Juggling gunshaft
　　　　And spear in one hand, unsheathed knife in the other,
　　　　　　　Unbalancing on one leg
　　　　　　　　　In two feet of water—
　　　　　　　I'm struck from behind

　　　　By a six-foot wave I didn't
Hear building over me
　　　　From the left, the wave silently purring a surf-lip
　　　　　　　As the crest curls down in a fist
　　　　　　　　　Of foam—to pounce
　　　　　　　With cat's stealth: I hear

　　　　A cracked-whip's impact before I
Recall it is my side
　　　　And neck that echo back; taste blood in the salt
　　　　　　　Before I know my lifestream
　　　　　　　　　The one opened, and on
　　　　　　　The run—escaping

　　　　Smoothly as into a love-sucking
Mouth; see a black fin
　　　　Slicing the surface and circling toward me before I
　　　　　　　Register the terror-sound
　　　　　　　　　Of flippered feet
　　　　　　　Wedging between coral

        Jaws to brace the mindless
Trunk they swing upon
        Absently, my legs a lever, bending against the back-
            Wash of the wave's undertow
                Pulling seaward to meet
            A next hammering wave.

        Shark-meat! Half-aliveness will eat
You alive! On all fours,
        I scramble ashore.... Now in dreams, I sink into brainless
            Stupor, a carcass emptied
                Of self, a drifting
            Deadwood, a flotsam

        Of absent flesh: my legs two
Shanks of floating
        Sea-fodder, my arm-bones crossed sticks under a death's-
            Head skull, my eyes looking
                Out through a death
            Mask of face.

II. Whelk Hunter in the Staghorns

In the low tide,
heavy surf batters the natural breakwater forest
                of antler coral, thousands
                of many-jointed crisscrossing arms
            reaching above
        the briny surface, absorbing
shock after shock,
shielding my suicidal roosts — an occasional high-lipped
                breaker overtopping the staghorns —
            as I pick my way between
                low inshore coral
        ledges, scouting for whelks.

A mere seven-footer
is a killer wave here, thinks the human crab, crawling
                on ice-slick shelves, terraces
            of stone, creeping and paddling

    by turns as the water
  level rises and falls.
Knees and forearms
slipping on the flat-topped silkmossy rocks of the inlet —
      half sizzling in the bake of sun,
    half awash in foam — I dodge
    the exposed horns
  of dozens of coral elks:

Sea-moose! My eyes
fastened to my wavering footholds, as I stalk, catpawing
      from footing to delicate footing;
    my neck in a half-twist, I take
    nervous side-glimpses
  of the far-to-near oncoming waves,
but my eyes fail:
they miss the signals, the worst wave hiding its froth-curl
      in the undersea ground swell.
    I must learn to hear the hiss
    and suck of the undertow,
  to feel in my shanks the least

tug of the backsliding
shallows, to sniff and detect fear-smell as it wafts
      from my epidermal radar:
    All warning systems alert!
    The water below
  my rest shelf sinks dead away,
I follow the least
trickles of wet seeping into bottom-mud craters,
      and the gliding shadow looms
    overhead. *I must cling like a leech*
    or be dashed to a pulp,
  my belly flat to a wide stone

slab, my four limbs
crab-claws hooking around the spiny ledges, tucked under,
      my back braced for the churning
    blow. . . . After the wave passes,
    I continue to clutch
  the boulder, pressing my gut

                    into the lifelines of stone,
            sensing in each rock-ripple millenniums of water-carved
                                intricacy. Slowly, I begin
                        sliding forward, all my life
                        flowing into my belly,
                my back strangely emptied,

toughening into a senseless
rind — all one piece — a curved bone-plate like the univalve
                        shell of a whelk or conch. . . .
                    Hugging the coastline, I swim out
                    from enclosed bay-mouth
                over deeper water beside shore
cliffs: flat slabs,
sheer planes of rock-face, steep walls of natural dikes.
                            No footholds or handrests here.
                            No arm-lifts for swimmer, weary
                            or seeking hideaway
                    from shark. No narrow trails

for shore-rats, mongoose,
iguana. A barrenness not to be scaled by wild rock-clinging
                        vines: no earth deposits
                    for climbing ivy-shoots —
                        tough, leafless,
                and rubbery-flexible — to take root.
Firm lodgement only
for quick-scurry lives, all crack dwellers: shellfish, creepers
                        of pit and rock-pocket. Trigger-quick
                    landcrabs, soft-bodied, light
                        exquisitely poised
                on legs that can tighten their grip

on stone sheer as glass,
rocking up-and-down, quavering: most skilled amphibian! —
                    nimble-kneed landcrab, straddler
                    of rock, wind and wave, loving
                        to survive on the edge,
                    perched for the breaker's chop.
Or rock-sucking whelk,
sliding just over or under the waterline, stranded

        too high on rock ledge if the tide
      recedes too fast, becoming fixed:
    frozen to a grave
by sun-dried salts: tiny rock-knob!

III. Moles in the Whelk Nest

Along the sides
of a coral-wall, many shells kissing the falling waterline
        abruptly emerge, sliding upward.
    I can hardly believe their numbers.
      Careless of injury,
  I leap into ten-foot-deep water
hunting the source.
Moiling plankton and bubbly froth-clouds block my underwater
      sight. My gloved hands probe
    and slither along sandy contours.
    Eyes in my hands.
    Mind's-eye in my fingertips. Drop off,
gloves. Fear.
Fear of sea-urchin spines. Long black needles that sink
      deeply into flesh, break off,
    leave irremovable splinters,
    dissolve slowly
  for months. Much pain. Swelling.
My fingers searching,
fondling the slime, threading through eelgrass and moss,
    sensitive to textures, to smallest
    faults or clefts. *Fingers stroking*
    a woman's fine hair,
  the sides of the fingers — not only
the tips — learning
the kinks, the flowing tress-silk. Deciphering in love-dark
    the stiff single gray hairs
    from the resistless soft blondes
    and browns. Caressing
  the coarse bristly hank of curls
over the genitals,
as springingly alive to the touch as flesh; or the soft
      thin down on the rim of the ear,

                    the earlobes. My knuckles gouging
                        into pits and sockets,
                    wedging into interstices of the reef,
tracing lineaments
and burrowing into all declivities. My hands tunnelling
                        like underwater moles, hunting
                    orifice — the aperture into secret
                    wombs of the coral.
                At last, my left hand drops
into a deep hollow
taking my arm in behind it to just over the elbow and lands
                        on a close-knit pile of rocks:
                    roundish pebbles, stacked one
                    on two or three
                others, spreading out downward
in a pyramid, the bottom
layers containing larger — the upper layers, smaller — ovals.
                        Whorls and spirals of my fingerprints,
                    think for me! Note finely etched ridges,
                    wavelike crests,
                at short intervals, elevated
on the surface. Ah!
Familiar shapes. I have invaded the secret nest of the whelks,
                    a family of shells in luxuriant
                    embrace, a community of mollusks
                    all connected,
                lip to back, content in a multi-
leveled architecture.
I start prying. As if drugged, they spring up into my hands
                        loosening in threes and twos, oilily
                    slurping together — now lip to lip —
                    as they fall into my net.
                The nest runs deep as a lode
of metal ore,
I, a blind miner, with bare fingers for shovels and picks,
                        knuckles for sledgehammers: the meat
                    in my skullcase, my ribshell meat,
                    my gutbag — all hungering
                for the gummy wormmeats of the whelks.

IN PURSUIT OF THE ANGEL

I. Wing Plumes of the Thief

Late afternoon. One hour before sunset. The water level
— sinking slowly away —
exposes the crowns of barely submerged
coral heads, altering the unbroken flat plain of offshore shoals

to a museum of pinnacles and arches,
alternately bulbous and square-skulled statuary
jutting into the bay,
solid replicas of the few cumulus thunderheads spoiling the pool-
pure azure of fair skies . . . I mount
the upreared convolutions of brain coral, amazed at my sudden
heaviness, as, stooping,
I creep on gloved palms and flippers, wary
of scraping knee or elbow (the merest scratch is a wound!) —
then using my speargun as cane,
I hobble upright on a flat center promontory
stretching tall, tall,
taller — for all my knock-kneed wobbliness — than any mammalian
biped, and wave my arms, squawking

to my snorkeler-*buddy*, face-down, gliding between two star
coral reefs, oblivious
(in another galaxy!) to the instant sculptures
jewel-studding the surface, as he weaves a zigzag path, foraging

for shellfish — lobsters, crabs,
molluscs — in hollows of the coral. From vantage
of my aerial perch,
he grapples between the furrowed gap-toothed jaws of an alligator,
the great notched maw is closing,
but the corrugated fish pail afloat in the inflated truck inner tube
wedges those gums
open and breaks the bite, tugging the nylon
draw-cord tied to his weight belt. He spins around to check out
the snag, grins at the clown

                    poised on one leg, arms spreadeagled, sashaying
                            like a model: together,
we behold the arrested aviary! The hundreds of birds, circling
                        and diving all day—bunched over

crisscrossing and interlaced schools of mackerel, gar, jack
                            and kingfish moiling
            in the choppy waters just beyond the surf—
have come to roost, poised on the coral shelves: the pelicans

                    float on their feather-cushioned
            haunches, comatose; the gulls and frigate birds,
                            slightly bowed over,
wings folded, stand in obeisance to spreadwinged erect cormorants,
                    black-bottomed muscular swimmers
that chase underwater prey: now, in peacock-spanned grandeur,
                            they extend waterlogged
        plumes to dry in the sun. . . . My reign ended,
I drop to a squat. The nearest shag leans forward, dips
                —wings outstretched, unmoving—
approaches a belly-flop, then flaps both wings, heavily
                            dragging its tail
in the water, and snatches a half-alive plump queen triggerfish
                        from our exposed bucket! Kicking

and splashing with his wide flat feet, a running takeoff,
                            he ascends. I jump,
        rubber webbed-feet first, into the shallows,
replacing the canvas cover . . . *I rescue the fallen wing plume.*

II. In Pursuit of the Angel

The horizon's wide ax-blade cleaves the sun's disc: poised hemisphere
                of fire, hung aloft, floats
for an unearthly long moment, windless,
    as if choosing between sea and sky, shrinks to less,
    less—a least flare dwindles, dies. *It is a pureness
    of vanishing* . . . The constant five
        or six rows of surf, alternately humped wave-

        backs and foamy breakers, have shifted
           from inshore shallows
              to the bay's perimeter, as if flowing wrinkles of sea
                  surface carpet were smoothed

to the far end of the rug. Now belly-floating, just beyond
                        the sand bar, indolent, I
idle in thirty-foot-deep clear water.
   Iridescent glitter on sea-floor shells looms near,
   detail of bottom flora as starkly visible
     as my hand's magnified knuckles.
       Everything in view seems within arm's reach,
       but fish grow scarce in this calm
         transparency,
            and squatter birds are thinning out, casting about dreamily
                toward the roiling food-chain

cycle waters of the bay-mouth . . . Memory. *I back-stroke six hours*
                      in my mind's eye rerun.
See again the direct stark light of midday,
  blinding at high noon. Sunny or overcast, the glare
    on live and dead particles — minutiae — thickens
      to an opaque wall of murkiness,
        impenetrable as dense fog. I feel
        suspended in liquid cotton.
          Partial clear-ups
            are worse. The bottom looms close, sways out far. All surfaces
                tilt, weave from side to side.

Objects teeter, warp — they lose and get back their shapes. I must
                      squint, or shut my eyes, often
to stop the vertigo and nausea.
   But now, in this twilight saliency, eyes touch
   like fingertips: sight extends the body, stretched
     nerves threading the water — seeingness
       grows its own skin, sensitive, sensitive!
       I drop slowly from the surface,
         letting reverse
           gravity and my free fall momentum balance, reaching
              a stillstand, for moments,

then slipping down some inches. Halfway to the bottom, I drift,
               musing, past a bouquet
of anemones, their many tentacles
   waving slowly. I touch one petal-shaped tuber,
   and the whole colony of blooms shrinks into tight buds—
      my eye recoils, a stunned flower
         itself, puzzled at the vanishing blossom
            quantities of atomized
               anemone. I
            stare and stare. They do not reinflate! . . . *If all distances
               seem close up, what happens*

to up close? I force my eyes to focus nearer, the effort
               to adjust my irises
like switching binoculars from mountain
   skyline to shoelaces and blond leg-hairs. Scanning
   minutely down lengths of my forearm and spear
      gun, my dilating pupils clamp
         a few cubic milliliters of plankton,
            scrutinizing the carnival
               gala. Minuscule
            acrobatics whirl in refracted light, the tiny lives
               spinning upon themselves—

dazzle to dim, sparkle to fade—dancing and effervescing,
               luminous as fireflies. . . .
Near bottom in the shallow inshore basin,
   I'm lured by rainbow-flash of a queen angelfish
   and swim toward the drop-off beyond the outer coral
      reefs, settling downward. I descend
         along a slope, cruising parallel to sand
         bar's steep gradient. Diving fast
            with my back and hips—
               flippers undulating, hardly moving a limb, I circle
                  the fish for visual feast,

nearly colliding with a wide high-backed flat sheet of tin.
               It turns to face my advance.
The sudden narrowness of body,
   in front view, magnifies the bulbous eyes—a spadefish!

Nearly circular, it measures perhaps three feet
   in diameter, more a shield
      or skillet than a shovelhead: so wide
      and gleaming in profile, queerly
         tubular head-on.
            It swims, by a succession of nervous rushes, and hair-
               trigger turns. Soon, it is met

by a fleet of thirty or forty spadefish, mostly small fry,
                  swimming in formation:
largest members, near the front and middle
  of the ranks; the smallest, around the periphery,
  a few not able to keep up with the school.
     Broadside on, they wrest my full
        horizontal compass of vision — I must
        rotate my neck from side to side
        to take them all in.
           If I release a shot at them, wildly, how can I miss
              hitting two at a time?

I try to single out a large target, but I lose tracery
                        of separate outlines.
They overlap so much, I can see no gaps
  between them: a mosaic — continuous —
of interlocking tin fish-shapes. As I fumble,
    taking aim, a stout front steersman
      pivots into reverse, and the whole colony
      turns with him, swivelling, folded
        upon each other —
            though none touch! *A shuffler's trick with a deck of cards.*
               Halfway into the turn, all

catch the light at once and emit a single blinding flash!
                  Now in the rear, the helms-
man chases the group. He pivots again.
   Bizarrely, the others follow his rearguard lead.
   Still puzzling over the odd chain of command,
      I accidentally fire a spear.
         A frenzied blur. Fish are scattered, hurtling,
         in all directions at once. Spot-

light bursts! I blink,
again and again . . . *As swiftly, the dozens of loose cards*
fly back into the deck.

III. The Black Holes

The school of vexed spadefish sweeps in a parabolic downward
curve — luminescent blade
of a great scythe cutting a wide deep sea
swathe — and drops out of sight. *Swift evacuation!*
I am left with so much just-emptied space, a hollow
waiting to be filled. What is holding
its watery breath? It seems that I'm surrounded
by a great collapsed lung, dreaming
the next inhalation.
Can the vast sea choke on its own deflatedness, drowning
in a short-winded void?

Bubbles, bubbles rising! Detritus falling, filling the black
holes, a constant thick rain
of live and dead matter to lightless depths.
My eye zeroes in on minute diatoms: tissue-bits,
thin beings — slender threads of life raining down
from the surface, never to touch
bottom! The many frail sliver-lives, cut short
in mid-fall, are food for bottom
feeders . . . *Oh constant*
gift of nutriment falling from genial skies of upper sea!
Nothing starves! Nothing starves!

THE REGATTA IN THE SKIES

I. Ago Bay: The Regatta in the Skies

1.

                For hours, our Pullman (half sleeper,
        half parlor car), crammed with vagabond backpackers
              and holiday executives,
burrows into denser clotted passages of Ise-Shima National Park,
            the woods often crowding the tracks
so narrowly we seem to be boring a tunnel as we advance, pine boughs
              and foliage coalescing
        behind us.... Flashes of blue glitter, to our left
and below; the woods thin out; stretches of aquamarine run together
            in a continuous unwound ribbon flanking
our descent to sea level—the parallel band grows wider,
              suddenly leaping alongside
the tracks and flowing, at last, in a bright tributary below us
            deepening to turquoise, bottom rocks

glinting in the shallows. We climb a short overpass, our tracks
            an elevated scaffoldwork
      flung across trestles, and we burst into the clearing,
forest walls falling away on both sides in a swiftly widening V

        at our backs. Ahead, we bisect
    a long isthmus—propped on our raised causeway—yoking
            the wooded land mass
to a narrowing funnel of pasturage. *Goats and calves graze.*
      A stray bull lopes up to the train,
springs back with a grimace, horns upraised for attack.... Water
            to left and right,
     all woods left far behind—a shrunken blur—
we seem to gain speed as we traverse the contracting strip
         of land, hastening toward land's
       end, our destination, Kashikojima, the town
            fixed to the tip

of the peninsula, a great jetty curved like a boot toe to fit
                    the looping contour of shore.

The train seems aimed to overshoot town, docks, the coastline
                    mishmash of urban
         and nautical traffic — our engine may vault
the lovely outlying islands! . . . Spray from Ago Bay, saturated

            with scents of pearl-oyster beds
         and Nori-seaweed, floods in upon our nostrils — and now
                flowery jasmines, lilacs,
sea-grapes, as the wind shifts. Mountain breezes give way to sea gusts
                billowing up from the bay. We advance
to the forward car, maneuvering to view the approach to Pearl World.
                An island-studded seaway
        rushes to meet us, the miniaturist color-engraving
on a postage stamp of moments before, pulling us into its ballooning
              enclave. The maritime scene expands
        into a panoramic bustle of countless land and sea vessels. . . .
                Exiting from the train,
I check my footing — the platform sinks a few inches, pitching
                this way and that. Seaweed tufts —

sweeping across the city-long quay, blown in eddies,
                commingled with lines
        and cables of ship moorings — now settle
on the multiple decks of tri-leveled luxury steamboats. . . .

2.

              Passing under one low arch
              of railroad viaduct —
at right angles to the pier and dock-yard — we seek out
                the buried hamlet.
We thirst for contact with townspeople,
        the local populace! . . . Scouting for an urban interior,

        we track uncertain footpaths
            up a steep hillside.
The summit, a broad mesa, stretches to the horizon —
              silhouetted on the sky,

    a few marshmallow cloud puffs, rushing
                to keep pace with jibs and spinnakers, match the sails

            for size; flanking the low trim hulls,
              the cloud balls unravel
tails and tatters flaring out behind them,
                      their sister-sails intact
but forward edges luffing from time to time
           in the strong headwinds. Cloud and canvas ride

            the same fierce currents. . . . We stroll
         across the raised
plateau, arm-linked, enchanted by the regatta
                  in the skies. The bay surface,
dismantled by the sun's glare, grows
        invisible. We advance for a detailed view — the sea,

            a mirror now, doubles the fleet
                of clouds into two tiers,
an echelon above, twin echelon below.
                  We behold the spectacle
of white spheroids, ruffled quadrilaterals,
          and cupped triangles converging — amassed and fluctuant —

            upon the horizon. Ascending into a bloom
            of thunderheads, banked
and swelling in the East, the whole galaxy
                    of vessels and frayed cloudlets —
airborne — swept past the quartermoon's
         pale crescent, flies higher and higher. . . .

II. The Roof Tableau of Kashikojima

      An hour's uphill trudge leaves us milling about
    on the flat-topped peak of Cape
Goza, more weary of matchless sea gorge,
    overhang and declivity than shrine
      or Buddha. Absently, I
        glance across the peninsula —

I'm brought up short: Kashikojima-shi,
   the hidden village,
      is stratified at all levels
   of a forested broad foothill,
      oddly globular — topless pumpkin! — far side
rimming the opposite coast.
Shifting features of a lit Jack-o'-lantern's
   carved face, hinted by gleams of ceramic tile
      roofs, wink successively —
         sun's glare shuttling through gaps
            in passing clouds. The dwellings are scattered
               at various sites
            of hillslope: near ground level,
         the lowest stratum comprises
      a few geometrically-shaped, gray offices
   interspersed with modest huts.
Those bungalows facing the sea are graced
   with gallery or portico; the foursquare
      lodgings facing inland,
         diminutive, bare, are stripped of all
            outward appurtenances. Halfway up the bluff,
               we discern in wooded
            groves a pair of *Minshiku* —
   half inn, half private home: the seaside
   commercial wings are provided with second-story
balconies; while the domestic
quarters, colorless annex to vacationers'
   charming hostels, are boarded shut —
      a castiron latch fastened
         over each close-fitting set
            of stout cedar shutters. Near the hilltop's
               uppermost strata,
            a posh *Ryokan* abuts —
         elegant tile-roofed verandahs
      at each floor level. The inn's base, on a downslant,
   slopes across a stratified
cliffscape of terraced gardens, four stories
   visible on one side, six on the other,
      perhaps two or three
         underground levels to house
            the hotel staff: quarters for maidservants,

≈ 100

    landscape artisans,
     chauffeurs, aristocrat geishas. . . .
   Scanning the whole hillside —
  from top to bottom — my eyes suddenly bypass
  the eclectic diversity
of abodes: I exult in a common glory,
  shared by one and all — the panorama of roof-
   tiles! A rainbow mosaic
    of countless shades and colors,
     the design or pattern wavering as sun shifts,
     darks and lights vary
    with the fluctuation of cloud
   masses, dimming or blocking
  the sun, by turns. At a given moment
(as a succession of frames
in a color film of the roofs we still view
  today quickly reveals), one variegated
   scattering of tiles — which cuts
    across many roofs and catches sun
     at a sharp angle — softly heightens the colors,
      producing a foreground
     of brightly glinted shapes.
    Animal episodes. Flower
   bouquets. Human profiles not unlike faces
  glimpsed in the clouds. . . . Or the eye
swerves to the background gestalt of tiles shaded
  by the sun's obliquest angle, undertones
   of muted colors — diamonds
    and tiny parallelogram flecks
     shuffled and reshuffled in a swift unfolding
      of suaver images,
     but no less vivid a flux
    of emblematic portraits from life. . . .
   Or, in moments of idle witnessing, the eye
  fumbles — a blinding flash drowns
all color in glare! A mirror-sheen of tiles —
  few in number but fatal in brilliance —
   reflects the light, blazingly.
    It coerces the viewer to blink,
     or glance to one side. . . .   Our film captures
    each configuration

          of the shifting tableau's
        alchemy, in turn. I find,
    if I slow to a halt the flow of celluloid
through the projector, I may catch —
in blurred frames — the rare moment! All three tile
  mosaics spring into view, at once, coincide,
      and form a montage: each figure
        glows in an independent plane,
            claiming its own distinct niche in the spectrum
              of visible light;
        the display of colors — in each —
    projects a dominant hue,
or nuance, set off from the others; yet they merge
and blend in one composite,
the ghostly flux of the movie screen. Now one
  appears to leap closer to the viewer —
    while two figures recede —
      now another, the mobile field
        of tiles passing through the two stationary
          planes, in each advance
        and retreat. Interplay, or clash,
      between the varicolored tableaus —
  a triptych montage — reveals the unearthly beauty
of this hillside township
as in a timeless, fourth dimension. . . . Today,
  our film commences, anew, to uncoil
    from its slender reel taking
      us back five years to the hour
        we first stood on the broad mesa, and viewed
          Kashikojima's
        brilliant festival of roofs:
    the indigent cottages
and huts, frugal chalets (twin *Minshiku*), posh
imperial villas
and drab offices — all sporting, in concert,
  ski-sloped roofs, overhanging eaves curving
    upwards. . . . *Hands of a troop*
      of subaltern gods reaching out
        to catch the rain, fingers upcurled to embrace
          whatever manna falls
        from skies perpetually charmed

    by the visual Mardi Gras
     of tile displays checkering the unbroken sweep
   of circular landscape,
  tiles of all shades glittering around and around,
   alike in pale sunset pastels, halftones;
    midday sheens of gold;
     or morning riot of greens, blues,
      reds — bold wholetones: a hillside cornucopia
     of color ablaze!

III. The Sea Caves of Dogashima

1.

      We arrive in mid-day,
    by bus. Hefting bags and satchels, we can hardly
stand upright in the wind, great undeflected sea-gusts battering
     our flanks. I cannot make out
     the landmarks of town,
  a blinding hail of fine gravel and dust catching me
     full in the face. Lifting
     the long wing of my poncho —
a cape to shield my eyes — I cross the highway for views of seacoast.
    Hunched at the guardrail, I linger on an elevated
     bridge . . . Before me,

     a dense archipelago
   of isles and reefs, interspersed by constel-
lations of tiny islets — the larger bodies oddly mushroom-shaped,
     puffy and bulbous in the high
     middles, eroded and undercut
  around the borders. Each ballooning island, shoreless —
     a weave of verticals — juts
     skyward from the seaface, buoyed
on a sandstone mottled neck just narrower, at the base, than crusts
    of overhanging rushes. The mushroom tops
     seem to sway

      above the stalks — whole
    islands teetery over the wasting pedestals,

                natural bulwarks lifting them free from heavy swells and pounding
                            surf. Each upraised land mass,
                                teeming with birds and foliage
                (its luminous silhouette delicately etched on the mist),
                            flickers and flutters in the cross-
                            currents of transverse wind gusts.
Now shimmering in the silver-blue haze and rose-glow opalescence
                    of twilight, the great inverted chandeliers,
                            endlessly branching,

                            scatter radiance beyond
            measure — each island, a mirror-image of the town
upborne . . . Dogashima.
                                Town on stilts!
                                        Undulant city, rocking
                on trestles!
                                    Population adrift
on a boardwalk-wharf, quay of stone blocks and knotty
            planking: a floor to the town,
                to beach, a slatted roof. Dozens
of long sloped ladderways connect shore to village, ranging from one
            to four flights as the coast falls away, slants
                    into the horizon.

2.

                        Several ferries,
                sighted from the small balcony of our private
Ryokan overlooking the beach, circle Dogashima Bay from dawn to dusk —
                    each follows the same deft route,
                    a zigzagging switchback course.
        Three craft in view, each at a different phase in the winding
                    seaways labyrinth, negotiate
                    intricate sharp turns and arcs
through straits between islets, or narrow canals into sea-caves,
            tunnels bisecting natural rock cathedrals.
                    The small vessels,

                    queerly vanishing
                into the hidden sides of apparently solid
rock-knolls, beetle out the opposite end, moments later. Or they emerge,

startlingly, from the entrance —
exiting bow first. They maneuver
with the adroit surety of a team of one-engine skywriter
biplanes swooping into cloud-banks
between words . . . High caves, notched
like windows, fleck one island's peak. A gull, swiftly cruising, pierces
the slotted apex — fleet passage through the stone
pinnacle's needle eye!

3.

A short step down —
we file, bouncily, from dock to upper deck
at midship, the children spluttering *arigatos*, rudely bypassing
the proffered helping hands
and ceremonious bows of kimono-
draped fellow passengers . . . I descend in a babble
of apologies — ours and theirs —
rival choruses, spanning
whole octaves on the melodic flute-scales of Japanese politeness.
Reciting forms colloquial and elegant,
by turns, I spin about

on my heels too late
to scold the children nimbly dancing
along narrow ledges — two on portside, a third on starboard —
approaching the forecastle, swaying
rashly over the oil-blanketed
water as I fantasize leaping overboard for the rescue.
The monkeys, snickering at my shouts,
land safely on a loose plank-seat
high in the bow (hardly a bench!), flanking the shipmaster. I,
withdrawing aft, fall into a low proper seat . . .
The multitude follow

the skipper into the glass-
enclosed cabin, below. *Do they desert the choice
deck-quarter to escape a demented foreigner, pallid father to harebrained
louts?* . . . Chugging from the pier,
we take a wide arc to center
of the inlet mouth — the one wide stretch of waterway

                in sight uncheckered with land-
                    shapes. Skipper cuts the engines . . .
Two masked heads, surfacing, dart into view off starboard. We all sweep
            astern to witness the divers lobbing the large
                    oval spiralled shells,

                    tinselled with seamoss,
            into the floating bucket. I time the next dive —
two minutes! The men, master divers sporting ageless physiques, haul in
                    scores of prized *awabi*, hourly,
                    from seafloor rock-shelves
            one hundred feet below. Lifted over those muscly shoulders
                    for overhand tosses into the wide-
                    rimmed barrels, the abalone
shells' mother-of-pearl lips flash milky iridescence in the sun. . . .
            Picking up speed, suddenly, we enter a maze
                    of narrow passageways

                    between countless low-
            lying oblongs and a few large hump-backed raised
muffin shapes, marshy and lush. We accelerate, again, churning directly
            into a floating skull-shaped edifice
                    of sheer unbroken stone, void
    of all vegetation. It raises its vast protuberant brow
                    higher and higher over us,
                    casting its ghostly elongated
shadow across the prow and spreading aft as we approach, never veering
            from our beeline collision course. The whole ferry,
                    at last, is swallowed

                    in suffocating blackness. Now
            we are standing still, the billowing rock-face
charging toward *us*, its bulging forehead bearing down from above . . .
            Almost too late, we swerve right
                    and slacken our speed; gliding
        around a narrow projecting lip, we follow the perimeter
                    of the island's base — just beyond
                    the bend, a great wide mouth opens
above us, yawning over our heads, and we come about, retarding
            to a slow sputtery putt-putt. Then we steer
                    into an apparently boundless

                    cavity—a geode's hollow?—
            expanding between rocky jaws of the island . . .
a moment of grim darkness followed by a play of lights and shadows
                on cave-walls of a widening tunnel.
            The reversed funnel-shape opens
        into a colorful display of greens, yellows, grays: a light-
                show flashing on the walls and ceiling
                of a natural amphitheater—or chapel!
What the source? The water below, refracting light from distant star-
            coral reefs? Or portholes in the rock, hidden
                    from view, but admitting

                    fat rivers of light
            like projected beams, unstoppable and piercing,
of a high-powered searchlight—lightstreams hurled into the cavern,
                tossed back and forth between walls
                    of the tabernacle, and dispersed,
        burying the source? . . . We drift, pivoting, and arrive,
                slowing to a halt in the center
                of a wide circular pool. Storms
of light—a sudden amazing brightness!—pour down on our upturned
            faces. We stare directly overhead into an oval
                    hole gouged like an eye

                    of Gargantua clear through
            the island cave's stone roof, exposing a naked
ellipse of cloudless sky. Many long vines, tendrils and creepers
                of ivy, are suspended like eels
                    dangling from the rim (a wild growth
        of lashes from the giant's lower eyelid). Now the eye
                begins to turn, slowly, a clockwise
                    spinning—I hear twin motors
perk up, rumbling, and I know it is ourselves in motion, again,
            revolving in place about a fixed axis, stationary
                    under the peephole

                    zenith. Flaming sun
            pops into the gap, a fiery white-hot pupil
crossing from left to right. I stare at the flower of fire, squinting.
                The blossom sends forth flares
                of bloom, unbearably bright flame-

tongues, radiating outwards from the center. As quickly,
             it dances away — smarting our eyes
             like a solar eclipse (no time
to flinch), then leaving us to blink away intense pained after-images
             exploding under our shut eyelids: Roman
                     candles spouting balls

             and stars of fireworks.
         Shading my eyes, I peer through narrowest
eye-slits. Two large insects, at opposite corners of the giant eye,
             rotate around the edge. From one,
             a spider-like arm unbends, dropping
a small morsel toward us trailing a long twine — it splashes
             into water adjacent to our craft.
             The other waves an appendage,
as if in greeting. My son waves back. *The view unblurs:* two schoolboys,
         leaning over the rock-orifice, dangle bait
                 from long drop lines

             for fish. Grown inured
to the befuddled upturned eyes of ferried
tourists, as to the angry grunts and scowls of the ferrymen, the anglers
             melt away into the rock-roof,
             their arms and legs blended amid
wind-tossed ivy tentacles . . . Exiting the sea-cave, we swing
             wide to make way for the next ferry —
             stealing a single backward
glance: the boys, now straddling the island peak's sunlit crown-fire,
             wave farewell, flapping carp-pennants
                     overhead in the wind.

≈ 108

THE GRAVE RUBBINGS

                Perched on one
           leg, pale egret atop a rock,
              arms outstretched
     for balance—less bird than scarecrow!—
I hover on the summit of Kashikojima Bluff, and praise
          the late, indolent ruddy sun,
    squat pomegranate poised over Ago Bay. . . .
            The children, long since
    drifted off with their mother, meandering
           to a downhill plateau—
their zealot voices, echoed in the distant gulch, break
              into my reverie . . .
       I scan two or three pine groves
        stratified on the downslope
    beneath my hilltop ledge, hunting their plaids
      and colorful stripes; absently, I
focus nearer—and catch a glimpse of three backs—figures
         lying face-down, scattered
            on a wide ridge
        directly below: they look
           so close, spied

   through field glasses, I feel as if I can place
    the flat of my hand between my son's
     shoulder blades (he nearest, stationed
    just under my lookout—I lean and sway,
neck stretched over the mesa edge for the view) . . .

          Each child, prone
      to a flat slab, limbs sprawled
         in various postures:
      the boy leaning on one elbow,
one of the girls supported, tripodlike, on the left knee, left
       elbow and right sneaker sole,
     she swings her free arm from side to side,
         a stroking motion—

all three children are kneading
(with some tool or other?)
on the rough surface under their legs and thighs. . . . I proceed
down the path
advancing toward them, keeping
the glasses focused
on their labors, noting — in semiprofile —
they straddle wide sheets of paper,
no foolscap but firm-textured quality leaves of drafting bond
begged and secured from mom's
favorite sketchbook,
black handprint smudges on Isaac's
chin and temple,

long smear across his forehead — telltale splotches!
They wield soft sticks of charcoal, brittle
and crumbly, black flakes of Carla's stub
of snapped char-stick spotting her skirt-
hem like soot, or dye, small chunks flying away

from her clenched
hand as she scrawls . . . *bits*
of hard ash spat
from embers, or hickory coals
ablaze. . . . They cannot be sketching freehand likenesses
of local flora, game
or wildlife, since they never raise their eyes
to check out a model,
nor take the measure or scale
of a subject. Strokes —
drudgelike! — are drawn in a to-and-fro plodding rhythm.
Long sweeping lines.
No pauses for accuracy or sharpness
of detail. Pressure
constant, tempo unvaried, their brusque moves
a motion of polishing or sandpaper
scraping — more the act of one smoothing rough surface
than suave strokes of Creator
of Life Studies.
Semicircular wavings. Systole.
Diastole.

The heartbeat of windshield wipers. Oh my angels,
my creative brood! At last, I pop
the question. "Rubbings, Dad," in chorus
comes the reply. "We're doing rubbings
of tombstone art, story-pictures of local sights . . ."

I survey
the wide oval cliff-recess:
half of the chosen
acreage, city-zoned, is hidden
under cliff-overhang; the other half a wide plateau-ledge
visible from my former lookout
vantage, above; outer limits marked by two
high red Torii gates,
towering in front and rear, shaped —
I always fancy! —
like colossal models of the Greek letter *pi*. This haven,
adorned with scattered
statuary, is less a graveyard
than open-air museum,
the handful of headstones memorial sculptures —
a few, statues of civic heroes
or saints in local town history. The stone monuments comprise
two pentagons, one octagon, three
wavy ellipses curled
like Calder mobile hangings,
any number

of long rectangles, a few upended to heights
of ten or twelve feet, most lying flat;
two towering figure Ls; one Mitsu-
bishi emblem: three triangles spaced
in a circle, each triangular concrete block

welded to the two
others by lengths of steel tubing;
one high pyramid
perhaps at dead center of the grounds:
the two-dozen-odd steps to the top shelf, thick slabs
of concrete, are graduated in size
from twenty-foot-square base to platform apex

affording footroom
(with little space to spare!) for two
of my junior clan
who, having raced each other to the peak from opposite sides,
are now pushing
and shoving in a king-of-the-castle
contest. Each, claiming
sole possession of the castle keep, tries
to drive the other from the tower
fortress. Scaling the pyramid steps before I can devise
apt verbal threats to fit
the occasion's hazard,
I descend, two turncoats clasped
by scruff of neck . . .

Older sister, aloof from ruffianly sibling
squabbles, persists in her rubbings,
crowding into a single wide sheet
of drawing paper a carnival
of images transcribed from many tombstones,

in succession.
A wiry she-goat scuttling
on all fours
across the flat-topped octagon, she hops
from one to another of three conjoined Mitsubishi triangles,
winding around the rim of an S-
shaped ellipse; now balancing on the narrow base
of an L, arms
and abdomen draped around the edge
of tall L-throneback.
Scouting for rare finds, she fills the curled page margins
with exact replicas
of script *hiragana* and *katakana*,
Japanese alphabets,
each a handsomely detailed total portrait
in its own right, much-curlicued,
derived from Chinese ideograms. The perimeters of her page
are neatly crammed (she ever
the orderly child,

obsessed by tidiness to a fault?)
with lined-up rows

of characters — each coupling two or more pictures
into a single alphabet. The page
corners and foot-wide borders are stamped
with large line drawings of local shrines,
historic belfry, pagoda, and temple buildings,

a few sites
instantly recalled from our *unguided*
quick tour through town,
the upright originals we'd passed
much simplified in the few lines and spare markings of grave-
stone embossments . . . Now she moves
by design — as if following a charted itinerary
through hallowed grounds
of the classic dead heroes and ancestors —
to the tallest rectangle.
Holding her work-in-progress up high against erect marble
with one hand —
palm pressed flat, she starts marking
and shading with the other.
Tranced, she works over a large raised portrait
jutting out from the surface — embossed
to thicknesses of a half-inch, or more, details textured,
acute (or so I discern, standing behind
the budding portraitist —
not making a sound, but peering
over her shoulder) . . .

Eyes luminous, she is filling out a large center-
piece of her canvas, the empty space —
a wide circle she left in the middle — saved
for a select masterwork; many smaller
rubbings distributed around the vacancy, a few

squeezed so close
edges touch, or corners overlap.
Alert to audience,
she slows her pace, finds means

to control the balance of lights and darks in her shading,
holding the full length of char-stick
sidewise — flat to the page — for lightening. She marks
with short quick sweeps
of the chalk's blunt end, etching
succinct dots and stripes
free of fuzzy smears. She is developing style, a fine art
of rubbings. But the spiel
she gabbles to her eavesdropper parent —
palaver of truisms — dissects
expertise at rubbings, as if she'd foreknown
the whole repertory of skills.
Yet I can read the glut of discovery in her eyes: surprises
of touch, her fingertips' supple finds —
sensory illuminings!
Response to sudden caprices
of medium. Flarings-

out of a new intelligence gushing into handprint
whorls, wrist-reflexes, fingerjoints:
a chalk flattened against digit knuckles
slides into wispier flourishes (arcs
and swirls that adorn light shadings) than finger-

ends afford;
extended index finger guiding
long line-sweeps
better than leading thumb.
This miracle of mating handrhythms to medium is *her being* now,
this new artifice she rolls
and slicks over the page. *The moves starting up*
from her hip and spine
as she dances flowing brush-strokes
of the soft powder-stick
into the midsection of granite. Or shoulder-floats and dips
her downstroke
into the solar plexus of limestone.
Or hip-swivels and grinds
her side-winding cross-stroke into lumbar vertebrae
of a little rich marble column,
with only the flat thin sheet of wood pulp epidermis gliding

between her pale smooth skin
and coarse hewn rough
stone skins of the lurking beneath
grand dead,

their body's last gristle and integument sighing
back to half-breath in her sneeze primed
by wind-blown black chalkdust snuff
or tickly pollen. . . . No way did a father's
gift, last birthday, of rudimentary homearts paint

kit prepare her
for outdoorsarts of tombstone
massage and rubdown:
"No talent, and no art, Dad. That no-win
toy . . ." Dimestore number-map paintings. Rote sloppings-on
of pigments. You follow strict equatings
of number-blocks to prescribed colors. No color
blends allowed. Fit numbers
to colors, colors to numbers. Pat
match-ups, all . . .
Her secret. She lifts her eyes, often, as if seeking hints
for this scenic rubbing
beyond the high squared limestone death
tablet she labors over,
and beyond, even, this cliff-ledge graveyard
(part recessed tabernacle, part
broad mesa)—a distant reference point to which she returns,
again and again, as to touchstone
for testing details
of the incomplete rubbing: a rock-
studded seascape

(the exact contents of the scene eluding me,
prior to this moment—now the broad
outline emerges intact, at last!) . . .
She tries to hide her stolen glimpses,
furtive. *Tossing her long bangs out of her eyes?*

Or easing a neck-
quirk? But these gestures are faked.

I can decipher her far-
to-near pattern of squints:
following each half-veiled stare in the distance, she reworks
hairsbreadth fine details of wrought
charcoal. . . . So I study the scene portrayed,
both familiar and strange —
it depicts a classic sunrise at sea,
the sun's opulence
wedging a cleft between two huge whaleback-shaped rocks
closely juxtaposed,
a narrow strait, or channel, flowing
between them. The true sun —
at this moment setting behind us — casts
an ashy vermilion glow
over the many sky-piercing memorial stones, silhouetted
on sea and cliff-backdrop.
She never looks back
over her shoulder, whether to glare
at the parent-spy

crowding her easel-stance and blocking the last light,
or to steal views of the broad prospect
of sunset on the opalescent sea-tract
at our backs. No model of the sun
(in ascent *or* descent) having caught her eye, I search

the anterior skyline
horizon for images, images to match
her secret borrowings
and glosses on the original *text*
of the nature-study in raised relief on the tall stone's face . . .
Ah, *beautiful thieveries!* The wedded
rocks of Futami spring into view, just visible
above the high left scarp
overhead — lurking a little outside
my line of vision
while I hang suspended, fluttering over the able draughtswoman's
locks. Now, stooping
to inspect minute details of her craft,
I find myself sharing
a far corner of her perspective, the stark view

of Futami dodging into my vista.
I follow the long thick straw rope across its hammocklike swoop
and suspension from a topmost front edge
of the high rock-island's
slanted cone to the egg-shaped crag
of the lower isle,

and I insert a mental picture of the famous sunrise,
the squash-colored vast disc passing upward
between the rocks, filling the cleavage
(cork stopper in bottle top), as in Carla's
near-to-finished rubbing of Futami. *The top arc*

of fireball
in ascension is stalled parallel
to a wooden Torii's foot —
the great tall pi-shaped cypress tower
anchored to the large island's peak, lording its full height
over the sun in stasis of art's deep-
freeze. The slack straw rope, bisecting the solar
orb (a drooped ring
of Saturn?), marries Futami's two rocks;
the tattered annual yoke
replaced with great ceremony each January 5, those rock-island
mates symbols
of Japan's two mythic creators —
Izanagi and Izanami. . . .
How well she knows she improves on the engraver's
handiwork! Hurrying now, she races
the dimming light, conserves the last sun strong enough to work by
(mirroring the mind of the scene
portrayed, she'd freeze
Sol dead in his celestial tracks
for the half hour

it may take her to finish) . . . Now adding frayed straggle-
ends to the rope, and daubing traces of halo
aura to the rock-island crowns, she conjures up
flickerings of the haunted presences
of myth trapped incarnate in the sea-whipped rocks. . . .

JOREN: THE VOLCANIC FALLS

1. The Detour

   No time to ride the tram-car up the precipice
overlooking Shimoda Bay,
   where Commodore Perry flew the first U.S. Consular
flag in Japan . . . No time
        to read fine print under rocks and sculptures
        in the Museum of Phalluses,
      erotica
   masqueraded as art and geological prodigies . . .
      We mill around
   a far-flung central bus stop, junction of bus lines
      to all points
   of the heart-shaped peninsula,
      north, east or west: a sprawling bus-switchboard
with dozens of outdoors terminals; behind each,
line-ups of waiting passengers.
   After mistakenly filing in three long rows,
we connect. *Coast Highway closed.*

   We shall detour north up Mt. Amagi, cross Mt.
     Amagi Pass, then transfer
        back to sea-
side. . . . Cruising slowly across the long low valley stretch
      inland from coast
to foothills, we speed up, capriciously, on the first uphill
      curves.
   Wheel-ruts and chuck-holes
roughen. The driver, rural kinsman to manic
       Tokyo cab jockeys, edges closer and closer
     to the road's Continental-left side,
     which vanishes beneath us.
                I leer dizzily
   from the left-rear window, hiding
my winces from the children. How do we find room

                to dodge the occasional
                           motorist
bearing down on us from above with no warning on curves?
           No shoulder.
                          The moldering
road-edge borders the cliff.
                           What prevents our wheels
                from sinking,
                   plunging us into the gorge?
           How is it the driver's bold fast moves

    negotiate the gravel-run's ducks and swoops.
I can see a direct plumbline
    down the precipitous overhang—we are flying!
Bite down hard and hard
           on my fear   open me to the exact beauties
                   of the live flowing valley
                           rippling
    and shimmering   a river of grasses and leaves and tree-tops
              flying below   spilling
    into a long iridescent tunnel of our going   fanning out
                       behind us
                   streaming away... We loop
              a grand circling mountain dance   a spiralling
upsweep:
                   bus   road   cliff   valley—
                                      revolving
and careening all together: no swerves!
    The whole valley breathes our heaving and swaying
course— our moves the mountain's breath....

    Swoosh!
                   The bus lurches right, bucks,
              taking a high bounce,
                   rear wheels
upraised for a full three seconds.
                              My sucked-in breath
              explodes, the killed road
rematerializing beneath our axles. Now we are riding
              flat and level.
              A conspicuous sign flashes

    our altitude in meters: the last rise
            we floated across is the peninsular apogee —
       Mt. Amagi Pass!
                We coast,
         skirting a ridge suspended over a double-crater
         valley, so densely wooded
    I can barely make out in silhouette the family
        of extinct volcanoes that lived
        and died here.
These defunct craters spawn teeming legions of forests,
        mammoth ferns, high grasses,
wildflowers . . .
             The road, narrow ribbon nestled between two
        rows of hills,
      bears a sharp uphill left.
We halt. *Dogashima junction.* The bus empties.

2. The Descent

Three hours stopover. Last bus to West Coast.
Shall we risk the long hike down
    the steep earth-crevasse to Joren Waterfall?
We stroll to the edge of the ravine,
           hover on the upper lip of a downhill trail,
              a serpentining pathway.
              Voices
    approach from below.
                Three slender figures in kimonos —
        two women and a man —
emerge, advancing slowly in a zigzag course up the sheer
        incline;
      one woman, trailing
        the others by a short gap, braces each second
step with a bamboo cane.
                She jerks to a stop.
Eyes shut, hand cupped over her nose,
    she whiffs immense slow breaths — in alternate
snorts — through each nostril, drawing

                silent vast power from the atmosphere. *To breathe*
                    is the art . . .
                                How far down
                        are the falls,
we ask? One hour, the man replies, bowing from the waist.
                We all bow and bow. . . .
Warning the children to follow — not lead! — we descend.
            I test
                each step, noting the irregular
            pattern of man-made stone shelves, terraced
                        ridges, notched and indented in the rock.
                I mark the slipperiness of gravel,
                    the skid-risk of oblique slopes — stooping,
                my knees close to earth, I stalk,
        grasping rock-knuckles, tree-limbs jutting
            over the path, or latticework
                intertwining
vines and lovely flowering shrubs.
                                Two rabbits scurry
            underfoot. I trip over one,
trying to snatch the other. Debra spots a fawn, leaping
            from a cliff
        overhead, its white furry tail
            vanishing into a small cave-mouth. At last,

    we take turns passing each other on the narrow
single-file path. A wind
    I hardly noticed (fanning gently my left cheek)
shifts and gusts, shoving me
                from behind!
                        How does wind velocity build
                        in this gulf, fissure,
                            deep earth-
            rent, gouge, rock-enclosed mountain crevasse?
                            I retard
                my steps to a halt too fast,
        lean back on my heels, and crouch to keep from falling.
                The children
                speed up, their heads

               and backs rolling in a downward spiral
     below my legs   disappearing   reappearing
around bends. *Such grace and poise*
   in the rhythmic sweep of wind-lashed limbs!
Beautiful, their absent pitching

       of hips and calves! How lovely the mindless
         unmindful dance I missed,
            too self-
bewitched, caught up in my own dream-gliding trance.
       Surefooted, they caper
and sprint as small animal paws — all weightless ease —
          scuttle.
       In my long ten second
    lapse   space! space!   so much free wideopen
         floating invisible being
                         Oh how I listen!
        I can hear my underfoot heel-
          tapping and small branch crackling die out.
        The wind-whine, tickling my neck,
quietens, dissolves into a bass two-octave-lower
       sigh-absorbing rumble, ahead
       and below:
a distant gurgle too evenly dinning to be surf washing ashore,
    a sound of water
flying in wide slender sheets, water caught and wailing
        as it spreads
          into a tower of falling churn —
    suds, lather and froth — diffusing to spray

  at the misty perimeters: the falls, the falls!
We draw near to the chasm floor.
  I pursue the runaway children — lunging,
I stumble into a soft gravel bed
               at the foot of the winding path, half-tripping
          into a wide oval pool
         of dark blue
water, so shatteringly clear I can see a few sparkly bits
        rotating at depths
    of fifty to a hundred feet: a crater pool — or bottomless
            abyss? —

                    many times deeper
            than wide, deeper than the distance around,
    deeper than the steep high whirling wall
of water that empties into its mouth,
    tons of wetness plunging from the canyon
roof, hurtling its body of mountain-top

        apocalypse — a sky-fire-keen howl of downgush! —
            into the serene instant-calm
                of the rippleless
level poolface: the silvery raging belt of churned-up foam
            tearing itself apart, wetness
shattering, ripping itself inside out, eating its heart
                out to become
        scud — weightless, bodiless —
to fight free of the bonds of mass, gulping
            air-pockets in mouthfuls, feeding on substanceless
        ether, absorbing more and more
            of the floating sun-laced life of bubbles; swindled
        by the mountain's lie, the summit's
promise of harvest into airborne vapors, a reward
    for falling, falling, falling
            to its cease,
exhausting itself in a mighty impact on the pool's stony face . . .
        Distrust the lure
of innocent leaps, bounds, hurdles. Fear the trigger-impulse
            of the child
        within, of the child in all.
    Where are the children? Have they been whisked,

    resistlessly, into the drink?
                    I cry out, stunned.
The girls — their voices muffled trills —
    answer.
            They are entombed, locked in the wall
to my left, the gay replies muted,
            filtered through thicknesses of volcanic quartz.
                Echoing resonances. I leap
                    across bulrush
    to the wall, start to claw the children free from a cliff-grave
            with shredding fingernails.

Can their small bodies fit around this bare smooth rock-surface,
             slightly arched —
         I ponder, tracking with my palms?
     The ledge at my feet answers. Two short zigzag
   steps across the lip of a shallow cave
glide me into a high long cavern.
   I follow the pool-edge trail, a narrow
overhanging ridge, and join the girls —

         transfixed by a view beside the falls. Squinting,
            I make out dim outlines. *Take
            two steps. Refocus.*
At the far end of the basalt cave, I secure ideal sight-access!
         Slowly, I translate the placard
posted on the cave-wall:
                     *Buddha-image behind falls named Jizo.
             Guardian deity
       of small children. Carved
   from natural rock by Kobo-Daishi. First Shingon
             Buddhist in Japan.*
                     Balancing on the cave-ledge,
             we lean over the pool rim to peer
                 at the lofty fine chisel-work of the priest,
             the gentle curvaceous face and shoulders
   looming above us from the twenty-foot-high
             Divinity carved in shallow
         relief,
indenting the rock to varying depths, sunk to a foot or two
             in elongated gaps
framing the cheeks (hovering, neckless, over wide shoulders)
             and columnar
         thick biceps; below,
   his delicate turned-in hands resting on cross-

   legged lap, the fingers upcurled, knuckles
and thumb-tips of both hands touching,
     each to each: in *Mudra* position, hand-symbol
of sermonizing.
             From our perch, the falls
         drape the Buddha diagonally, half-blurred
             by the shawl of falling

                    water,
            half-clear and distinct.
                        We try to visualize the brave sculptor-
                    priest stretching his gaunt
            lank-fasted frame slenderer on tip-toe to keep from toppling,
                        sucked
                    into torrents of the water-
                wall just parallel to his back, and flung
        headforemost into the pool-side granite!
Now we see him mounting his makeshift
    scaffold of woven osiers and vines, climbing
the wickerwork ladder toward the high

        great creaseless forehead and intricate marbly
                design of the noble God's
                    corona.
We see him chopping and battering the wonderful half-shut
            eyelids shaped like butterfly
wings, his elbows often grazed by the churning water
                behind him—
            adjacent to his heaving shoulders
        wielding the primitive hammer and stone chisel—
                    sending a charge of hydroelectric power
                    into each of his swings.
                                How happy
            he is, the magic voltage of the falls roaring
                into his limbs, animating his whole
    skeleton with a power like fire—fire born
            of water; his slim frame
                seems to shed
all remains of flesh, exposing a radiant luminous bone-
    tree.
                He shudders and quakes
with love-toil, hovers as a candle-flame pants on its wick.
        "Kobo-Daishi,
        Kobo-Daishi":
                his name on my lips,
    a gasped murmur, rises to prayerful chant,

        the girls winking. (Impish snickers.) I point
    to the statue,

     "See him there, watch
  his swings! Oh how he dances hammer-blows
into the stone, the sparks flying
      all around his flushed neck and ears, a galaxy
     of flint-sown stars doused
     in the falls,
  instantly reborn, showering from tireless blows of his stone
     hammer, dying out,
  born afresh each moment, constellations of fiery pinpoints
     of light —
    a frenzy of creation! —
   circling his voluptuous strokes."
             But they
  see a different scene, their yelps — barks
of alarm — shattering my spiel.
  Their truant brother, the family drifter,
reappears at the Buddha's base.

    How did he scale the steep rocky slopes behind
     the falls, daring to leap
      over a corner
of pool-edge, passing unnoticed by the rear approachway —
     surprising us?
     Trapped
between rival impulses to scold and warn him, I choke
     down my cries,
    and sink into the cave-wall
   at my back, dazed.
         He ignores us, squatting
    on the narrow ledge at the statue's foot,
   parodies the Divinity's cross-legged
    straight-backed posture, the blank stony
    stare and half-closed eyelids.
           Now he begins
  to slip down the slight incline of his roost,
    the seat of his pants
    and trousers-
legs sliding him toward the perilous junction of falls
    and pool.
     He tumbles,
half-losing his balance (no hiding the fear in his eyes),

                    rolls over
                on his side, and scrambles
        to safety—clenching his sister's outstretched

    hand, dancing and cavorting the last few
steps to simulate poise, control.
My hand, open palm flat to the cave-side,
braces my weight. I hold steady,
                    let the spinning lights slow down behind shut
                        eyelids, shortness of breath
                            freezing me
        to the spot.
                        The children's voices fade, thinning
                in the distance as they skip
        downstream, following the run-off from the pool outlet.
                    The shaking fit
                        falters. Quits . . .
                            Dreamily,
            I brush my fingers up and down, from right
    to left in widening circles, startled
    by the coarse texture of wall,
        varying in color from dark gray to black—
thinking, *igneous, igneous rock.*

    Fire-begotten. Fire-container. Glassy hardness
            repeats my pulse. Wall-rock
                thumps
with my stolen heartbeat, my blood flow thudding in stone.
            My lifelines—handprint whorls—
fight down terror, finding deep calm in the touch of rock.
                When Kobo-Daishi
            paused, dreamt between chains
    of hammer-blows, he knew this wedding of flesh
                    to mountain-rock, this union of opposed
                bodies to make a third, a vessel,
                    a medium, a mock-human brooding image:
                the Buddha Ikon:
                            a stone body
        inviting the great Spirit of the God to enter,
            to become enshrined, to inhabit
                    the stone skull,

        stone breast, folded stone limbs — with grace of touch
            the God enchanted by the man
to break holy silence, to rise from the mute invisible
                void and enter
        the avatar of body-form,
    engaging the man in a lordly dance of Spirit:

the human to be rewarded with eternal grace,
and grace to all who come after
by luck to this consecrated place of blessings
to children: safe passage, safe
            child-passage throughout life . . . Kobo-Daishi, who,
          in caves north of this gully,
              met and fought
        and subdued demons, then sculpted the rock-embossed body
              of the God beside the falls . . .
        Again, I pass my hand across the wall, sweeping from side
            to side. Tall
              wavy columns of basalt rock.
                No lava-slag. No vomitus from the planet bowels
    crater-spewn, leaving blanketed acres of live
topsoil smothered by black dross.
    No formless wild spatter of chunks. No coughed-up
clots of earth-blood . . .
                    My palms imbibe

    flaming masses of liquid earth, sudden rivers
        exploding between continental
            shelves
and shaped into wall-forms below the surface, the columns
        jutting closer and closer
to the planet skin, the mountain evolving layer by layer
            from within —
    a struggle to contain
    the swelling pool of fire.
                    My pulse is afire.
        I stroke this chilled rock-face, volcanic
        braille, deciphering by touch
            the fantastic blaze which melted the earth,
        the violent magma-boil tearing
deep cracks in earth's lower crust, molten

                    fire-rock thrusting upwards,
                              freezing
in place, quick-set and quick-shaped in formed columns,
                    earth's fireball center
sculpting and re-sculpting its surface outwards. . . .
                                        Here,
                    in this place
                    of change — midway sector,
               caught between form and flow, essence

    passing between shape and unshapen fluid,
this incision in cliff-side, this mouth,
     this great unstanched wound in world's body —
I read the peristalsis of her cycles.
                         Igneous rock. *Fire-born. Fire-swallower.*
                         Quick-melted, quick-set
                                   in the cooling
          of its own fires.
                              Ah! — *to contain vast inner fires,*
                    then to be shaped
          by effusions and wanings of the flames, riding the wave
                         of torrential
                    flow, trapping the blaze
               in marbly-veined shapely columns.
                                             My body's
    dreamscape! Naked border zone where earth's liquid
core and chilled crust meet.
     In this place of delicate thresholds, birth
is open wide, the kiss

     of deep inner fires still close to the surface —
               all transformations! All
                    fountainings!
Hot spring waters boiling into steams.
                                   Geysers spouting
          fumy sprays.
                    Liquid
rock bursting to the surface, crystallizing into minerals,
                         jewels,
                    and walls of volcanic
     glass.

The falls igniting into foam. . . .
                    Beachcombers, seaside vagrants, we chose lowland
            peripheries, but uplands chose us,
                    wafting us up foothills to summits, luring us
            down into the mountain's innards.
We voyage into *the gash* — exposed interior
        of earth's tender Mucosa,
            membranous
lining of her body cavities, her panoramic acreage of rock-
            viscera laid bare. . . .
                            I saunter
down the stream-side path knowing, as never before, earth's
            give-and-take,
        the recoil and snapback
of gravelly walkway, springy to footfalls.

3. The Whole Breath

    I meet the children dropping hook-and-line
            from handmade bamboo poles
                into the brook,
    run-off waters from the falls.
                        Fish strike the small
            breadballs of bait
    in midair, leaping from below, their tails kicking up
                little whirlpools
                on the surface.
                        The young men
    who lent the poles, reclining in idle poses,
            applaud, while the children toss their whole catch
                back into the stream — three bucketsful —
            each unhooked fish lively, flapping uninjured,
                the human sport a brief detour
    in their joyous cycle from mountain-top birth
                to valley streams, riverway
                to the sea.
Here, near the exploding falls, all life-lines between man
            and creature   connect,
    connect. Everywhere, the life of water   rock   fish   child
                sweeps

             from form to form: glorious
    interchange! — the alive of all terrestrial

  families nurturing every alive other One   by One
by One   the smashed waters dying
    at the God's foot   issuing forth from the sleep
of the deep crater-pool into child-
                    blessing rivulets: a place of healing!
                                        Molten rock
         boiling and burbling upwards
             from below,
  iron-heavy pile-driving waters flung down from the peaks above:
         this atmosphere, each holy
  influx of our dream-breath yawned from the wide free life space
             of Divine
         Breath — opening all around us
     like Mozart's celestial music — is fatefully tinged
  with a fragrance of commingled heights and depths
  a message that passes fiercely from breath
     into mind   held in mind's grip   as volcanic falls
in aged mountain's memory   are gripped

ODE TO THE RUNAWAY CAVES

(Ochos Rios, Jamaica)

1.

Approaching the caves, we shuffle
    down a long path —
  bark
and leafneedle bestrewn, our course winding
    between aisles of trees,
  criss-
crossings of thick vines overhead drooped,
    at times, to our knees,
  ankles —
we must take high steps, or crawl below . . .
    The taller pimento trees,
  skins
unscrolling like eucalyptus rinds,
    give way to palms,
  old trunks.
The thick boles — sickly, rotted — languish
    in the embrace of creaturely
  sidewinders:
trees sprung from sky like air plants, trees
    hung from the shoulders
  and necks
of quickly aging mates, draining the saps,
    sucking out the mineral
  enzymes. . . .
Anaconda and vampire!
                It strangles a donor
  tree even as it sips
  bole blood —
then stretches its many aerial plunger
    stems to earthward,
  puts down
stays for anchorage, and deserts the host —
    left to crumple, collapsed

slowly
into dry-rot hollows . . .
                      That distant cousin
          to the copious banyan — the fig,
    the fig!

2.

Corkscrewing down the long tubular stairwell, we descend
        sixty-odd steps
            of the spiral ladder
    (the steel frame inserted in the deep narrow shaft
in the rock, a natural chute affording passage to all
three cave levels), eyes
        of each riveted to the next footfall: the head
        of the Swiss child below, her locks
        bobbing just under my halt instep; two German
dowagers above — hefty *fräuleins* — bickering
    over the slow pace, floppy sandals
    grazing my brow, now and again;

our guide posted one floor below the thin floor we file through —
        gophers dropping
            down a burrow — grips
    each pilgrim under the elbow (the last step
is overlong), or he lifts the children down with hands
cupped under hips
        and motions to clasp, likewise, the twenty-year-old
        blond Canuck from Quebec,
    her eyes spurning his advance as she swerves — wordless
in her dodge — past his outstretched forearms: smitten,
    he turns in a crouch admiring her thighs,
    no one to break my shortfall,

I following the checked pass, my footing shaky . . . *Third level.*
    The lowest cave
        basement. Or may this floor,
ceiling to still another tunnel, collapse

     underfoot? We pause a few moments, letting our eyes
adjust to dimmed light,
         the few widely-scattered electric bulbs spaced out
         over the high cave roof. Zigzagging,
         feeble as birthday-cake candles, the bluish eggs cast
small patches of dull-gray glow on the ceilings:
    the light recoils, trapped in overhead
    pulsing ovals — it falls back

on its source . . . But now, the broad dimensions of our earth-
        cavity limn
        themselves on the black ink
impenetrable sea of rock far to the left
and right, and to a great misty distance ahead. We take
our first sheepish steps.
     The floor vanishes. It sinks under our footfalls.
     We seem to proceed, unmoving,
         against the black immobile backdrop. A shimmer-
halo capsules our troop. We drift, weightless,
    as if enclosed in a foamy nimbus
    of half-light, ellipsoidal

balloon that lifts us and carries us forward, so far below
        earth's crust we dream
        our limbs free of gravity,
    as if we ride on a satellite orbiting
    outside the atmosphere. Distant arched cave-walls loom,
hazily, into view
      (I think of low-ceilinged excavated walls of mines) —
      abruptly, we bear left, our guide
      leading us single file toward a pool of brighter light.
Magnetized, we are drawn into the widening lit
    circle — our invisible knees, legs,
    and feet refleshed. We duck! —

shrinking to elude a heavy flapping of wings overhead, one
        winged shadow-pouch
        hurtling so close to my face
    I feel its wind-puffs fanning my ears and wave
    my arms, shooing away the attacker. Then, we hear
wing-bursts zoom upwards,

        the blind flyers shifting their course to avoid us.
        Rockets! Taking right-angled turns,
    they dive straight into a gap in the cave-roof, the flood
of direct sunlight striking their outspread wing-tops
   with a near-physical impact. The bats'
   wings — braking their ascent

to an utter halt — shudder, as if so much raw brightness
       were a solid wall,
        the light's body thudding
heavily upon their backs — an invisible mass
weighing, weighing. We make out three or four bats, clumped
closely together,
     battling fiercely against the light-barrier, sun's
     gleaming steel repulsing wave
  after wave of their terrible failed climb, failed exodus;
we sidling near, the better to witness the air show,
   shocked at the size of the crumpled wings
   beating in place. Giant birds

of the underworld! Bats large as crows, Hades' blind offspring
       hang suspended,
        their black iridescent wings,
  sun-speckled, lost in a limbo of stuckness,
  heaving, trapped between two unseen archenemies —
sun and man, twin satans
     of bat-purgatorio. Then, by a common will,
     four angry black blots — shrunken,
    wings folded into nothing, buried in deep pockets,
buried in emptiness — plunge in perfect formation,
   divebombing our naked upturned
   faces, four guided missiles

diving as one. We flinch, twelve targets huddled as one, arms
       upswung to shield
        our eyes; and we crouch, back-
   stepping from the charmed circle of light, sungush
   pouring through the magic aperture — a circuit of slots
in three cave-roofs
       admitting a barrel-wide column of unimpeded light.
       Bravely, we shuffle the few steps

>   back into the lit-floor oasis. Hand-visors cupped
> over our brows (in mock-salute to Sol), we search
>   for hovering black lumps, or flung bulbs
>   swooping in vertical bat-trails
>
> amid traceries of vines dangling from out-of-sight trunks
>   or shrubs, anchored
>   to a near-forgotten sky
>   of earth-crust. Now we hear the bats zinging
> and humming, anew, in swift horizontal air-laps, wings
> grazing our necks and ears. . . .
>   Our eyes stay trained to the vertical wonders,
>   the guide tracing with the wand
>   of his index finger the outlines — looping up and down —
> of record-length stalactites and stalagmites,
>   two of the latter extending upwards
>   from the cave-floor, pinnacle
>
> vertex towering almost twice the height of the tallest man
>   in our party. One
>   inverted steeple — its spire
>   dropping to our waists — is fastened to a sunken roof
>   recessed in a thirty-foot-high arch topping the limits
> of our sight. The stone
>   icicles (all uppers *and* downers), fashioned
>   from calcium drippings, lengthen
>   at a speedy one-thousand-years-per-inch. But what
> are these tough cables, anchored below and above,
>   I ask, yanking quarter-inch-thick pipes,
>   lifting my weight on one by one —
>
> vines, stems, tubers? Figtree roots, split into many offshoots,
>   each hunting water,
>   threading hundreds of feet
>   through slits and burrows, attaching to damp surface —
>   they are glued stuck with a firmness of welded steel joints!
> The hardy fig — born
>   an airplant, a parasite — locks its long talons
>   of roots into a mature tree-mate,
>   dehydrates the host slow-sipping away its life, drops
> tendrils to earth and begins its second birth,

late trunks replacing the host-tree's
rotted corpus. And now we see

two long dangling fig-roots just overhead, looping and twisting.
    Blind snakes! Forked ends
       (tongueless, but on the scent)
  grope for fecund damp of wells, cave-swamps, cave-lakes,
  hidden breeding grounds, deep-dug to befit the ancient fruit.
Survivor. Mate-slayer.
    Master of the drink and drought, tough in stock, root
    and seed, your fruit is wholesome to eat —
  plump or dried, fresh-picked or aged, preserved in cellars,
forerunner to our modern date or prune. *Ancestor!*
    Lawrence marvelled at your manybranched
    slitherings over the bare rocks

of Taormina, worshipped that sufficiency in endless brood —
    able to beget
      ever more shoots of shoots,
  each root progenitor to families of others, others!
  But little guessed he this illicit netherworld root-farm
of the overland creeper,
    doubling its purlieu to above and below, the one tree
    versatile as a swarm of kingsnakes.
    And now two eyeless snake-heads venture forth, wayfaring
from a trunk earth-socketed sixty feet above,
    the tree's exposed top a mere fraction
    of its serpentining root-life.

3.

Drawn to a network
  of markings, dimly visible
  on one wall beside the sky-light,
we walk single file — stooping
for a closer look at the broken silhouettes.
    Bestial figures in murals?
At first, we avail ourselves of overhead light
filtering down
      through multiple layers

of ceilings and casting
faint glimmers on two or three nearest panels. Our guide,

at last, unboxes
    a trove of welcome supplies.
  Inching backwards, we follow survived
patches of line-drawings
down a narrow winding corridor, aided by candles,
    mine guttering in the small dish
cupped in my unsteady hand. The lower drawings, etched
in rock levels
        parallel to our knees,
waists, chins — no higher! —
are still finely delineated, some splotches of color lost

or flaking off,
    iridescent flecks winking
    on bordered profiles: dull orange faces,
antique brownish hides,
the few sparkles hinting outer limits of figures —
    man or beast — outlines faded
or blurred. A dull patina of color residues marks out
special features yet —
      eyes, nostrils, hair; blood flow
into pools, blood drippings,
blood coagulated beneath the torso of the just-slain ox

or wildcat. The men,
    portrayed, are squat and pudgy,
    their dwarfish stature divulged by waist-low
drafts of their cave-murals
(as measured against our own upright frames, huddled
    so close to walls we can sniff
crumpled pigments) — scene of the hunt, hand-to-hand combat,
feast-days: tableaux
      of Arawak tribal-art. . . .
We come to a blank
interval, and pause, groping for stable foothold. The space

between walls shrinks,
    but our guide bids us proceed.

    Soon, a pattern of starker images unfolds
at the level of our heads
and higher, some figures extending so far upwards
      only three or four tallest men
in our group can view, clearly, the topmost scenes: line-
drawings; the few strokes
        of this taller Race condense
detail, the contours
and shapes of creatures hinted by dotted outlines. Muscle arc

here. Lower jaw-line
    there. Thickness of line defines
    movement, collisions between figures, angle
of stance — a far cry
from the fine lacework of design and color palette
      of the pygmy Race who inked
and pigment-spattered the low murals we met before. (No one
knows, for certain,
      how old are the top-level
minimalist chalk
drawings: the style — lean and pared of excess — is signature,

I surmise, of Carib
    tribes who lived tens of thousands
    of years prior to recorded alphabets. Pre-
Indian cave-dwellers). . . .
Wait! What crawls here? What writhes across the walls,
    in waves? The whole cave-wing buckles.
The drawings leap! They shudder, twisting in the candle-
flickered tall flumes
      of light fanning out wider,
and dimmed, in the cave
upper reaches. The columns of light flare in and out (X-rays

of lungs inflated, lungs
    deflated), while the drawings sway
    from side to side . . . On the return trek,
I note a few incurved panels
matching up artworks of both eras, the one stacked
      over the other, a few inches
between the upper and lower murals — the newer scenes

  incised with care
    under their ghostly consorts,
so narrow the space
closing a breach of millennia between Races of cave mammals

(breeds of bipeds,
  both more or less upright). . . .
  The midget descendents — so many family
lifelines removed from Sires,
now rivals — fitted their neat blocked-out designs,
  minutely, below the counterparts
of Great Uncles . . . *Boasts or tributes? Did they fancy over-*
wrought detail-work
   and ornament superior
to matchless taut strokes
of their forerunners? Or did they guess their art outclassed?

4.

Blind bats, in greater numbers than ever,
  start zinging
    and flapping about our ears. . . .
We enter a wide central space, juncture
  where many arms
    of the cave honeycomb merge:
dodging those black vampiric swoopers,
  I slip
    on a curled wet leaf
(no banana peels here!), which quakes
  and slithers
    under my shoe-sole's graze.
I lower my candlewick. The footlong lizard,
  softskinned,
    is joined by two moist fellow
streakers, chasing each other up one wall,
  then zigzagging
    back to the floor (sides
puffing in and out, throats ballooning,
  at intervals):
    sure-toed and speedy

≈ 140

on wall climbs or floorscootings, segmented
    toe-digits
        visibly curling, uncurling,
little sockets perfectly fluid. Errless . . .
    Not lizards!
        Too puffed-up and fleshy.
Giant eyeless salamanders.
                Extra bodysize
    recompense
        for loss of sight? But blindness
is no curse in these unlighted vaults,
    not dungeons
        to those who — deprived
from birth of sky   earth   weather —
    combine
        the fluidities of runners,
swimmers, and flying beings into the one
    all-purpose
        slithery quickstep, a walk
that is half slide, half float . . .
                The fleet
of a dozen
        outsize salamanders
is followed by jumping blind roaches, thick
    as frogs,
        not stumbling on many overlarge
legs. . . .
        Now we traverse the longest tunnel,
    light-
        flickers on a pool of water
edging into view at the far end. Our guides
    recite
        lessons in speleology —
more intoned, or sung, than spoken —
    each pilot
        holding forth to his troop:
two clumped galleries, we advance, now,
    in a pair
        of loosely intact divisions.
Our three-quarters-mile circuit, we're
    reminded,

              is a mere token sampling
of seven miles of caves, gouged and carved
      by sea
            currents, the whole honeycomb
submerged below two hundred feet of water.
     In trance,
         we think our way back
to knives of currents and swells cutting
     the grooves
         and boring the trenches
in solid rock that became a labyrinth.
     Chainsaws!
         Hacksaws of all-eating
acidic brines and rock-piercing salts,
     corrosive
         to hardest quartz or flint.
A feat of rock-sculpture! . . .
                               Following
    the cave-craft
        exercise, the sea withdrew
(architect departed, but near his creation),
      survived
          by a second maze of six
underground pools, all interlaced, topped
        by "Mr. Lake,"
           dark pond we skirted past
at ground level, prior to our spiralled
      descent —
          the deepest lake in Jamaica,
its many subterranean outflows and runoffs
      funneled
          into the six buried lakes.

5.

    We step into a cavern,
the high-roofed iglooshape crowned
        by a dome — ceiling to a vast, oval, sunken lake
            adjacent to the narrow shelf

          we stand upon, hovering over the lake-
       edge to stare
         at our eerie rippling faces
              reflected in the glowing sheen
        of the lake's black mirror.
        Our stone footledge a pocked and cratered wharf,
  jetty of the interior?—
we dodge small tidepools scattered
      here and there, which — chants our guide — refill
          each dawn when the risen sea-
              tides lift the sunken lake, as well,
      to its morning
   high water mark.
             We advance,
        slowly, in bands of threes,
     to moorings of rowboats,
   two small vessels secured by ropes, the guides
each taking installments
  of three passengers for "a spin," a few
    circlings of the pool . . .
               Even as the first boat inches
      from the improvised dock, I'm lulled
          in a trance of recall: *when, in whose dream,*
    have I unmoored—
oars in the gunwales, rowing out
            from this ghost-pier to the center
   of a roofed body
of water calm as sheet glass? I'm hunting in memory,
  still, when the guide
tongues nostalgias of his fast friendship
   with the noble Scotsman, Sean Connery, formed during unnumbered
      takes for the few cave-lake scenes
           in the premier Bond flick, *Dr. No,* a Soul-
Brother love
  redoubled in later rehearsals
          for *Live and Let Die.* Now erect,
   he jabs with one oar
    submerged vertically, as a Venetian gondolier poles
a gondola from shore. . . .

                  *   *   *

The surface looks so opaquely black
    I feel as if our bow is a knife-edge, the little boat
        an ice-cutter slicing its slow path
            through ink-black ice, or through a slate
        of petrified dinosaurs
      and pterodactyls. . . .
                The oarsman,
            now stirring only faintest ripples
    in a flawless surface,
      drops one oar, taking up with his free hand a portable
spotlight (battery-
generator tucked in the handle),
      and points the projected beam directly below. He stabs
        to such depths so close to shore
            the very lake-margins seem bottomless,
      the light streaking
    past the limits of sight. But the lit
            column of water, so pure and stirless,
    takes on deep color,
      and we are cutting through green-black shale, milky-black
chalcedony; the light
a laser-beam drilling through stone
    or steel, with equal ease.
                Now he swings the lamp
    to and fro like a lantern — two slow
           swimmers pop into view at once, crisscrossing,
    the curvy snake-shape
      moving at right angles to the fish below,
            their even course not a trace deflected
    by the high-powered beam.
"Are they perfectly tame, or drifting asleep, if mobile?" —
inquires the German duchess
from Duttersdorf (sixtyish and mated
    to her coquette travelling companion, just out of her teens —
        nubile); the man at the oars, chary,
          who flirts with all women and a few
      young boys, demurs,
        addressing these two in deadpan voice,
            slow drawl pitched for a pair
    of neuters, or eunuchs:
      "No. Both blind," comes the reply. "Blind perch. Blind eel."

So saying, he follows
the snakelike glider to lower depths
   tracing the sluggish trajectory of its dive — his lightbeam's
      lazy-slow descent, a ritardando,
         paced by the droopy tempo of his spiel . . .
      Both species — scaly fish
   and snakefish alike — evolved over a stretch
         of lightless cave-aeons. Neither met
   by natural enemies,
      nor Killer-humans. Both protected, today, by strict Island
   Edict. Thus! Drift,
peaceably blind, from birth to death.
   (Feeding, no doubt, think I, on saintly blind plankton) . . .

     * * *

      A large crayfish, distant relation
         to the clawless Florida lobster, grabs
      the submerged oar-tip
   and starts to crawl upwards. It slips
         on the slick wood, straddles the edge
      with many legs pressed
   tight, now resumes its creep *down* the upward-pointed oar
   approaching the wrist
gripping its shaft — the guide showing off
   the blind crustacean's viselike grip and adroitness
      in the climb, descent or ascent
         all one to those hairlike antennae checking,
         blindly checking. . . .
      Four bats, chasing each other
            across the lake-face, charge
   the concave walls,
      the roof blinking in and out of the swung lamp-beam
   charting their wavery arcs.
Without slowdowns, they brake to a stillstand
   just inches this side of walls. Batswoops start and stop
      at full speed, arrow streaks
         the only moves those flung black blots
      think in their wing-
      bones. Far more exact than sight,
            bats' radar! No bats collide
      with panes of glass

                as sighted birds strike windows — flawless their skill
           in bouncing echoes. . . .

                              *   *   *

We are skimming faster and faster,
         our boatman racing breakneck into the cavern's rear wall
                    lacking batskill at sudden halts —
                         at the last instant, he plays a trick
                    with the twisted oars:
               we come about, a hairpin turn
                              as deft as a sailboat's tack in gale
                    winds; and we glide,
               hugging the cave-wall so close I can sniff the stone's damp
          coarse skin, my knuckles
brushing the moss and lichen sprouted
          therefrom. Our rower follows exact wavy contours of wall, fractions
                    of an inch between gunwale and rock
                              though he looks to the side, or faces one
                         passenger, another,
                    engaged in repartee . . .
                                   How does he keep
                         a parallel course, I wonder, never bumping
                    the undulant wall
               or swerving away? Does he, too, read the echoes, tutored
          by his bat-escorts
of two decades: men exchange messages
     with whales, dolphins — but not bats! . . .
                                        He drops both oars and rises
               to his feet, the boat not tipping —
                         come to rest in hidden nook. Odd music begins.
               He taps with his palms
          and finger pads. Cushions of his thumbs
                         look spongy-sensitive (possum or raccoon
          paws I have seen,
               exploring forage or nest-provisions with a touch
          so soft and feather-
light): he thumps, gently, on a wide,
     hollow stalactite, top-half embedded in the wall, bottom-half
                    suspended like an icicle, the shell
                         wavy, S-curved as if it housed a row of tall

>   cylinders or tubes
>   all connected.
>   *A series of organ pipes!*
>   Though his handpats roll lazyslow,
>   trembles of a bongo-
>   drummer, resonant scales that issue from the stone skins
>   mimic organ notes;
> his throat's guttural hums and groans,
>   in timbre with his palm-thumpings, knuckle-raps, simulate
>   organ valves, organ pedals pumping;
>   while the cave-dome is the great organ loft
>   in Chartres Cathedral.
>   *Eyes shut, I hear Gaston Litaize*
>   *command the instrument, two or three*
>   *dozen pipe-throats*
>   *all singing at once. Cathedral roof and arched cupolas*
>   *return matched counter-*
> *song in Saint-Saëns' orotund Third:*
> *echoes upon echoes, so paced by an organist, are the instrument's*
>   *cloak, its garment and accompanist.*
>   Cathedral and organ, cave-dome and stalactite,
>   wedded in duets —
>   voice of the first partner so woven
>   with the second, who can tell where
>   the blent song begins,
>   where it ends?. . . .
>   We are rowing again, glued to wall borders,
>   looping into hollows
> and tracing the stone perimeter
>   as if our bowsprit were a lobster's eye-stalk, tip of a superior
>   sight organ. But the rower looks away.
>   He lets the bow crawl to its own tune: "Old
>   Cathedral Rock,"
>   he intones, again and again, pleased
>   with his name for the organ-stalactite
>   he concertizes upon.
>   *He is naming a Spirit, his instrument shared with us. Voice*
>   *of the place. A personage.*
> We stop by a chain of long rock-icicles,
>   arranged in a pattern, roughly, of graduated larger widths.

        "Cave Man Piano," he cheerily dubs
            this unorthodox keyboard, and rolls the knuckles
    of both hands
      from side to side, the notes emitted
            mixing pops and tinkles and runs —
an upright xylophone!
    His tongue clicks accompaniment, completing a jazz ensemble.
One by one, we advance
to each new species of music sampling
      stalactites of all shapes and dimensions, each Christened
        with its own apt name: "Limbo Drum."
            "Rasta Roll Chimney." "Calypso Jim Chatterbox."
    We applaud each jewel
    in the repertoire.
              All jumping to our feet
          at once, we clap hands for an encore —
the boat nearly capsized,
    we drop in our seats with a great plop! Four vacationers' rumps
afford enough ballast
to restore our all-but-swamped vessel's
    balance. His recital ended, the maestro — too caught up in virtuoso
      songfest to notice we'd shipped gallons
           and gallons of water — now sets to pitching
    scooped bucketfuls
over the side, we frozen to our seats,
        the boat still asway.
              The two fräuleins,
    seated in the stern-bench,
    cup their hands together and ladle small palmfuls of spillage,
flinging the contents
back over their shoulders; too absorbed,
perhaps, in their frenzied waist-bends and heaves to notice
    that I remain still, if wide-eyed,
        jailed in a trance more active than hull-
    drainage furor. . . .

            *   *   *

          The searchlight,
    dropped to bowseat during the music solos,
        now switched to the dial's brightest setting
    in the scuffle, rolls

        to and fro on the bench, in time with the seesawing of the boat.
    As we drift, slowly,
back to port the power-beam flashes
    from wall to wall, roof to pool, pool-face to lake-depths:
        this ongoing kaleidoscope of lights
            and shadows meshes, at last, with the dim—
      but flickery—overhead
        one-hundred-watt bulbs strung out on wires
            hung like so many Christmas-tree ornaments
      from the lower roof
    topping the makeshift dock. The exquisite play of the lights,
    above and below, is magic
counterpart to the quelled festival
    of sounds, extinguished moments before, as if the echoes
        and multiple re-echoings of the orchestra
            of stalactite percussion family—drums, cymbals,
    timpani, castanets,
    xylophone—sunk into the silence,
            returns in another form: the lightshow
      before my eyes! . . . The ripples
    and small waves, stirred by our fracas, still radiate outwards
    from the lake's back end.
Our boat—stationed at the rear quadrant
    when we swamped the hull-floor—coasted, by a direct radius,
        across the long oval sweep of water
            shoreward; but the cycle of waves and small swells,
      touched off by our rocking
      and seesaw maneuvers, pursues our craft
            to its moorings and persists long after.
      Now wave-ripples catch
    periodic glares of the spotlight, whereupon the lake-face
    is floodlit, in surges,
like a stage show. . . .
            I'm held, transfixed,
    by tossings back and forth of reflections, the cave-roof aglow
        with mirrorings cast by the wave-pulse,
           confusing roof and floor.
                Stalactites and roof-craters
      change places with waves
      and splashed light-sparkles. Oval expanse
        of wet flickers over our heads, a lake

>   *ceiling suspended,*
>   *safely, thirty or forty feet above; while an arched stone roof,*
>   *reversed in concavity,*
> *is fallen below our legs. Our profiles*
>   *are cast above and below: heads and furrowed shoulders appear,*
>   *one moment, in a shuffled tile-mosaic*
>   *on the roof; our belt-buckles, knees, and sandals*
>   *glow, the next moment,*
>   *in a patchwork quilt collage on the floor*
>   *of wet spray, below. . . .*

6.

Back in line, my head still spinning with the lights bounced
to and fro between cave-
       roof and lake-face, we stall
for a long moment,
waiting for the two guides to choose between five tunnels
       for our departure and ascent
back to the sky of ground zero. The low chamber
in our rear, our gate
   of entry to the mushroom-shaped great dome,
   is joined by four other cave wings
which radiate

like glove fingers from the oval cavern. The bloated slow guide
chooses first. He leads
       his single file troopers
into the low-roofed,
thickest channel, the glove's wide thumb. In the few moments'
       delay before *we* proceed
to the narrower — if highest — tunnel (the hand's
index finger),
   the spotlight beam directed from the boat's
       bowseat, still oscillating, casts
a row of shadows

over the heads of those passing through the exit. Silhouettes
etched on the far wall

≈ 150

       loom tall as giants, lanky,
their elongated heads
and aquiline noses dimmer than the overbroad shoulders;
    while a second set of shadows
projected on the near wall by the string
of overhead bulbs,
     moving at the same tempo as the Race
      of Goliaths, exhibit flat
melon-shaped skulls,

thickset squat carriage, their legs oddly arched. They hobble
on the bandy legs,
        a Race of dwarfs. Their dark
shadow-bodies
look husky compared to the diaphanous-gray torsos,
     translucent, of their long-boned
twin brethren, the two Races of cave-dweller
muralists returned
    from widely divergent epochs. Their arms
    now upraised, members of each stock
wave a salute

to their kin! Two clans of cave-folk, apparitional, at peace
in the underworld, greet
       each other across mute Gulfs,
their grand meeting
ignored by the fleshly Race, trapped in their Chamber-
     of-Commerce Tour. Obtuse to forefathers
trading amenities filtered through our moderners'
witless shadows,
    our band of hikers resumes its lax pace.
    Before I can instruct my numb tongue
in words to share

my vision, I blanch to my hair-roots, sensing *my* hand, too,
raised of itself—unwilled—
      in salute to my cave Ancients,
fellow bipeds
snatched from oblivion. Perhaps their many lifted palms
    hold pigments, chalks poised to draft

more wall sagas . . . *Both flocks of shadow-folk halt,*
in lockstep. Hands
    lowered, they begin a retreat, back-
    stepping slowly. Then aboutface!
They all pivot

on their heels, and running in reverse, a few souls trip
on both walls at once —
      but it's the hikers between walls,
now in panic, who
return — crowding in their haste — to the long cavern,
    a woman near the front of their ranks
breaking out in howls, calmed to soft yelps by a help-
mate's pooh-poohings.
    The chain reaction of fright triggered a mass
    exodus, but all fear quickly melts
to laughter — while I

mourn for the sudden fadeout of both shadow Races, shrunk
back into the walls
      they graced in life with bison,
jackal, auroch,
and mountain lion, the same walls they flitted across
    for breathless moments of hailed
hand-greetings to fellows across Time. Those images
drown in the cave-rock,
    sunk as swiftly as the blind eels and perch
    which, crisscrossing our spotlight beam,
dove to lake depths.

7.

        Our Ace
    spelunker, still in titters over the Quebec
            blond's terror of the buzzard
fallen into the deep cave stairwell (her rescuer,
      himself), cheers me with whispered details of the fracas.
      The prey-fowl,
    its vast wingspread clogged and flapping,
           had ripped out wingtip plumes

in a struggle to free itself from narrow confines
        of the man-dug burrow (our intended exit chute); its beak
            blood-flecked,
  a trickle of blood dripping from its bruised
              bulb-head. . . .
                    A lame vulture,
overlarge, sickly, and old! But the City girl,
        seeing face droplets still moist (*gorging on which blood*
            type — mammal
quadruped or biped?), supposed the bird
              to be a monster vampire-bat,
a horribly enlarged mutant of the giant breed
        we'd met at the start of our hike . . .
                    Now both rows
     of pilgrims
follow their mentors, our smaller troop led
            through a narrow high passageway
to our chosen exit-hatch; and again, the shadows
        aflicker, I'm braced as ever to witness comings and goings
            of past tenants.
Our guide, taunted or dared by a wager,
                quickens our pace: a fast trot
escalates to a slow run, amid threats by senior
        spelunkers who feel trapped between fear of tripping
            in hidden ruts
and dread of being left behind for lost. . . .
              At a few gaps in our tunnel's
right wall, we're surprised to behold our companion
        line-up scuttling in a course parallel to ours; and later,
            I catch glimpses
through small portholes in the other wall:
              an obscure band of Islanders
four-to-five-deep, rudely bumping each other
        in their haste, are running in the opposite direction,
            their wider tunnel,
too, juxtaposed with ours . . .
                  Are they fugitives?
            Who are they fleeing? I, alone,
seem to notice the native runaways — hanging back
        for a peek at those in pursuit.
                In the eyes of this gang,

true agony!
Not for a moment, sport, or fake *angst* trumped up
to fool the lone peephole
voyeur. . . .
Do I recognize their costumes from drawings
or color plate etchings in Island history texts — the halfcaste
striped grays,
compulsory uniform of slaves?
My lord! The style
went out with eighteenth-century
sugar plantations, following the ritual murders
of three sugar barons, top-echelon slave traders. The instant
I decipher
the runners' style of dress, they vanish
before my eyes. . . .
Clippity-clop
of wooden clogs grows louder. Nearer. I clap hands
over my ears. The vacuum left by the disembodied black racers
doubles my pulse.
Ah! Their shadows, bare-chested now, are flying
over the walls, wave after wave
of runaways, their terror now mine. The shadows'
silhouettes so keenly detailed, I'll always remember three
or four faces—
those faces in dreams we've known all our lives
(or longer), but who? We cannot say.
That washboard corrugation of a tall man's ribs!
Stark receding forehead of the hook-nosed man. Those shadow-
figures hurtle
across the walls, again and again. Identical.
The same profiles, always running
in the one direction, never beating a retreat
or stopping for breath, the shadow outlines blurred, at last . . .
Bat runaways
veer, in formation, their squadrons zigzagging
in and out of the human fugitives'
shadows . . .
The refugees are running on a treadmill,
I fear, or conveyor belt always moving in reverse. It turns
at variable speed,
matching the pace of the runners, offsetting

       their escape, while they run in place.
But now, as I watch, the principals are changing,
    each new wave of shadows relaying a new host of actors:
      new vigilantes
  in the chase, new escapees on the run — for moments,
       in each wave, the figures chiseled
in luminous outline, their exact features knife-edged
    black on the cloud-gray backdrop.
            Incisive profiles!
   Columbus
and his brothers, invincible, laughing in escape
      with their plunder, crown jewels
and doubloons stolen from the British ships, smuggled
    through the vertigo maze of runaway caves.
          Now straggler Spaniards,
  last survivors
of the fatal gunboat battles with the Britons,
     steal back (through the network
of caves) to the one saved ship, hidden
    and camouflaged in an obscure cape of the Rio Nuevo, sanctuary
    just inland
from the cave exits. Later, they will sail
     to Cuba — never to return (today,
no Spanish in Jamaica) . . .
       Once more, the slave runaways
  appear, fugitives from British sugar magnates. Many, captured,
    will perish.
Others, biding their cave time, will migrate
     uphill into colorful mountain
coast ranges, so to found their own settlement
    of the sunken interior . . .
       Maroon Country.

SONG OF THE RIVER SWEEP

(Duns River Falls, Jamaica)

1.

               Apogee.
     The summit. Together, we've climbed,
               rock-tier by tier,
surmounting the last posted milestone
        to a higher overlook—Duns River Falls cascading
           in graduated
    shelves, light rapids spaced out
               over miles of slopes
terraced beneath our rock-tower vista
        affording, equally, views below and above;
            Seven Rivers—
resplendent!—traversing bluffs
               and rolling foothills
ranged as far as Eye's lassoings
        of visible horizon, the rivers cutting mesas and upper
           plateaus
into near-equal wedges. Commencing
              from diverse latitudes
of the Island's northmost perimeter,
        all seven waterway arteries and tributaries converge
           in the One
    Duns River passage—an oval bottleneck:
              calm as a lake, transparent,
poised over the plunging column of whitewater
       falls.
           The run-off, below, is abruptly squelched, foam
       levelled
upon scattered boulders. . . .
                  Downstream,
     a long human chain, led
by two guides, winds upwards, hands
        claw-curled in a forty-person interlock of unbroken
           links. Chain mates
    weave between the breakwater rocks.

                    They approach the base
of our lookout. Teetering on the rim,
            you pitch from side to side — a solo samba routine —
                    the dance moves
        improvised to match shifting grips
                            on your bulky Yashica
transferred from hip to shoulder, and now,
            arms extended, a two-handed thrust over your head.
                You reposition
        the camera's face for best angles:
                            shooting your wife,
your three fast friends, the linkage of hikers
            and waders threading — by cautious sorties — uphill . . .
                Now skirting
        the fountainhead of the strongest whitewater
                            falls, they duck and swerve
the last possible instant to miss a dunking
            in churned-up pockets.
                                It is a fencing match of parry
                    and thrust
        between the pliable string of human sausage links
                        and sudden gushers of foam.
A curling and uncurling bridge of bodies,
            stick-figures fused at arm hinges like clusters of paper
                    doll cutouts,
        this conga line-up of tourists gropes —
                            in leapfrog hops — from stone
to underwater stone, often climbing on knees
                over wide flat slabs, hands still clamped to chain pals,
                    fore and aft,
        the skirmishers reeling across the riverbed
                            in an undulatory formation
adjacent to the channel's West shoreline . . .
                Unseen by the safari of waders, a scattered work force
                    of islanders,
        many transporting large wooden washbuckets,
                            slowly traverse the downgrade
shallows of the East bank, nearing the leaders
            of the guided upstream hike.

                                        The native women, shirtsleeves
                    and long pantaloons
         rolled to the elbows and knees, pause to exchange
                              whispered gibes, snickers....
So we speculate, peering from our cliff-top refuge
               and observatory: do they not scoff at the host of vacationers
                    in polkadotted
         and beflowered swimwear?...
                    Middle-aged housewives
                         in widebrimmed straw hats,
moonlighters, they are stooping to scrub
         the overnight moss and filmy sediment from exposed rocks,
                    stepping stones,
         even bottom slates. They scrape off slimes, algae,
                    scums — rubbing all surfaces
with sponge, steel wool and wirebrush, their labor — daily —
         a race with nature to remove any slick spots. Indeed, they scour
              the very pebbles
         underfoot, peeling off slippery nocturnal skins:
                    they would restore coarse-grained
surface to all submarine footshelf, or handholds,
         to insure safe passage. Their diurnal maintenance of hikers' trails
              ebbs and flows
         in a lilting balletic rhythm, a dance cadence.
                         The river sweep's roundelay....

2.

     Three of the river scrub
crew break up into sport, at once,
     tossing buckets back and forth. Perched
on upraised mounds, they hurl large sponges — squash
     and eggplant shapes —
at each other's heads, a new mode
of water polo
modeled after landlubbers'
pillow fights. Their upriver fellow
staffers, an elder
generation by half, chide

the horseplay.
   Now the youngish matrons

   play tag: a short obese
walrus, hips wide as two shoulder
   breadths; her three taller associates
high-hipped and bosomy, rolls of waist flab
     rippling around
   all four midriffs . . . Fleet and agile,
   despite bulk, they wield
   their masses of torsos and backs
   from low rocks to high, as if flesh curves
   overlapping curves
   are stuffed with excelsior
     or cotton.
       Arms pinned to their sides,

   they logroll their bodies
in sandy shallows, much as lumberjacks
   birl the just-sliced segments of redwood
timbers in Eureka, California:
     all grins and teeth
   whitely flashing, their blubber jostles
   alike in water,
   stone, earth, or spray — at peace
   in flesh is their element, their skins'
   flow continuous
   with the life of surfaces.
     Who can say
       if their happy bodies

   first kiss — or are kissed by —
the foams? More porpoise than mermaid,
   lacking tail of a fish, but backflipping
and sideskipping like dolphins, they arch spine-
     rubber this way
   and that — jointless! Neck, thigh, pelvis
   swim in loose ball
   sockets, unhinged. All skin curves
   are piled upon curves until, fishlike,
   the human hide,

        unforked, is one curved edgeless
           pouch that slides . . .
              Brown womanlimbs asprawl,

      whatever falls is sun-lifted,
catches itself up like the waterfall
    splashing in their hair and eyes — all falls
playslips, all local fools playwise, sleep swimmers . . .
      The tourist line-up,
  strung out in a wavery double V, looms
  near . . . The native crew
  backtrack their rounds, so lightfoot
and prancy — Zero Mostel's rhino dance! —
  retrieved washbuckets
wrist-twirling, in time with jaunty
     long river-
        slicing strides of their climb. . . .

3.

So absorbed by the fadeout
   of the Ochos Rios bucket squad, I miss
      the sputtered cries of the chaperoned troop, now fallen,
         stooped in tangled
            factions of two, three, five — dislodged
from the buddy chain, none smiling, the faces in view piqued
     or aghast, a few
  dunked in spume of high spray or rapids . . .

Sampling the dispersed shuffle
  of aquatic hikers, hunched or fallen, I try
     to guess the cause of the spill, a farcical mishap
       that has thrown
           all members of the human chainlock
into offlimits flounders, sideline hobbles and gropings —
     as if a demon
  underwater prankster has pulled the rug

river-bottom out from under
  the scores of catwalking and goose-stepping
    folks (a few wearing expressions of aerialists toppled

                from a sabotaged
                        trapeze, irked, doubly, by the absence
        of net) . . . I hunt for a familiar frame in the blurred flux
                    of memory's ceaseless
            slideshow, but none fits the unique species

of pandemonium masqueraded
    before my eyes . . . One squatter, favoring a bruised
        limb, scans the river bottom for lost articles: an aged,
                    princely figure
                of a man, a great rolled tuft of white hair
        across his back rimming his shoulders like a general's silver
                    bar decorations
            for valor, rivaling the thick Irish moss

density of matted gray piled
    on his chest, but half-hidden from view as he bends
        from the waist; bending lower, he finally buries his face
                in foamy churn
                    of water — he grows too still for comfort,
        his companion poking him sharply in the ribs to make him raise
                    his head, undrowned yet . . .
            A roly-poly sunburnt Frenchman, fiftyish,

chases a tri-colored, striped,
    tall straw hat caught in a whirlpool, spinning down-
        stream (I delight to imagine the midget gymnast, submerged,
                who wears the hat —
                    puckish underwater racer, he dances
        frantic pirouettes: we suppose the hat madly twirls itself) . . .
                    The hat's tubby owner,
            hot in pursuit, is tripped — hopping on one foot,

he grasps the other and massages
    the injured heel, still reaching for the hat,
        which halts, then speeds up as he gropes for the curled peak:
            it always jumps,
                    just eluding his outstretched fingers'
        pinch. A blond teenager, dodging the hat chaser, gets wedged
                between two rock jaws;
            for a moment, she struggles in panic

as if the rows of stone sawteeth
   may clamp shut, a live riverbeast's obeah bite.
      Even at this distance, I can make out the angry red welts,
         skin embossments
            risen on both of her exposed upper legs,
   stings, I surmise, like firecoral lacerations; and now, howls
      from my one warm friend,
         your spunky wife tossing her tomboyish

short bob from side to side . . . I pivot,
   turning to warn you to go quickly to her aid
      when I spot your exact twin, below, springing up behind her.
         Your camera, left
            in haste and still whirring, lies on its side
   too near the cliff ledge, dumped, oddly, by that other you my skin
      and scalp tell me stands —
         if invisible — beside me still, my bones

not confessing your stout skeleton,
   escaping, escaped my notice . . . Puzzled, I lift
      the camera and switch off the motor, hoping to salvage
         some of the film
            left spinning on nothing — a patch of sky! —
   by your hasty exit. Now peering into the eyepiece, I adjust
      the zoom lens on the scene
         below: Marty, horizontal now, is upraised

on the stretcher of your extended arms.
   She appears to float on her back, levitating
      a foot or two *over* the surface, while a dark fleet figure
         approaches with stacks
            of gauze bandages (one of the older
   washbucket crew, so speedily returned as nurse), who, cradling
      heel of the injured foot
         in one hand, commences wrapping with the other.

I focus on the wound, the middle
   toe capped by a blotch of red where the whole nail
      was ripped off. I scan the makeshift hospital ward in midriver,
         from East bank
            to West, most of the departed scrub force

    reprogrammed, spontaneously, as a team of first-aid technicians
      armed with tourniquets,
     splints (sticks, metal bars), ace bandages

of all shapes and sizes; chemicals
  for swabbing scrapes and cuts (iodine, anti-
    biotic creams) . . . Soon, all the fallen Viking river-trudgers,
      back on their feet
       and smiling, join hands and resume
  their upriver trek . . . I linger, fondly, over the paramedical unit,
    a last idler, or two,
    sashaying a quiet retreat up the East shoreline. . . .

4.

       A giantesque
      thick-knuckled brown hand,
     pointing a direction behind me
    and overhead, crosses my lens —
   blotting out the scenario below (the pilgrim
   explorers, recovered,
  boldly heading into the teeth of the falls);
   and a lilting voice chants, so close to my ear
   I feel the breath on my cheek:
    a lesson in geopolitics
      and history . . . I follow the commanding
       pointer (hypnotic wand
      or baton) — it waves and circles,
    tracing the arcs and switchbacks
   of each river from its source on the horizon
  to its head, or juncture,
with its six mates in the lakesized pool, spread
  in unrippled calm above the falls. The hand,
    doubled now, blurs: *it is a twenty-*
     years-past hand traversing
      a ninety-foot-wide many-paneled blackboard,
       my anatomy Prof
     tracing the webwork of veins
     and arteries which converge
    in the human heart for a Med student rabble

   herded five-hundred-strong
in U. of M.'s colossal amphitheatre. . . .
  I'm awed, once more, by Island Earth's body
   vessels. Jamaica's rivers!
    The wide and narrow alike,
     the deep and shallow, the mud-opaque, the crystal
      pure transparent: all
     conveyors of prime life-support
    fluids, life elixirs, they pump
   their contents from the many distant river-founts
  commencing from seven
widely separate latitudes of sky, funneled
  back to the common basin — the Duns River heartpump,
   recycling the fetid, stale
    lazy-flowing gallon trillions
     through sieves and filters of churn-and-churn-about,
      purified and flushed
     into fields and pastures of harvest,
    then rolling into Jamaica's
   countless sea-kissed harbors . . . This forgotten glimpse
  of our Body's enchanted
web of rivers, channeled from every distant
  limb-terminating cell back to the grand fistsized
   pump, the tireless cyclotron
    in the left breast, returns in a flash!
     My eyes are held by the mentor's hand, my ears
      by her throat's warbled
     tutelage — in the brief instant
    before I drop the camera
   to earth, turning to face the long-necked sorceress
  sprung up beside me, there's no time
(nor respite in the riverflow of mind) to puzzle
  over her unnoticed swift climb from the cliff-base,
   by riverside, to my aerial
    lookout: she, the senior staff
     woman, eldest of the riverbottom unslickers,
      slime-removers, scum-
     scrapers. Yes, she was the austere head-
    mistress of labors I'd beheld
   in the rear, chiding her co-workers for their antics.
  Then, did she catch glimpses

         of the lone hanger-back, outcast or deserter
            from the swimsuited gallery, a hillperch snoop
               and voyeur? Ah, but taking me
                  for a student, or learner-aspirant
                     (armed with pen, scrawled jittery-inked notepad
                        at the ready), she rose
                     to my side, unbidden, to steer my eye's
                  passage and steel my sight
            river's meanderings of her particolored country's
         many-branched waterways:
streams, channels, creeks, furrows, canals — the whole sweep
   of visible outlands webbed and crosshatched
      with hairsbreadth fine threads
         and rivulets of water . . . She devotes
            her spiel to hand-me-down lore of seven great rivers
               conjoined in the Falls,
            her sage chatter a hybrid of myth,
         family gossip, anecdote,
      superstitions, legend and true Carib-history
   delivered in a lingo
blending equal shares of carny-barker's hype, streetsmarts
   and domestic patter — rhythmed in a lyric cadence
      of poetry. She was a poet
         extempore, an improviser
            of musical phrase, instant yokings of fact and dream:
               a singer of pictures!
            Now hearing I last sojourned
         in Sister Island Barbados,
      land of low-lying parched flat acres and drought —
   some parishes so dry,
arid desert compared to her country's lush slopes
   and vales — she rattles off lists of Jamaica's freshwater
      deep earth bounties. The names
         undulate with rolled syllables
            and liquid vowels proper to bottomless wells
               and unplumbed springs:
            redolent of tall tales she reports,
         boasts, of record-setting scuba
      and minibathysphere divers boring down, down, down,
   so many fathoms deep
the partners in science above — hugging the surface

    but tied to those brave heroes and explorers below
     by a code of tugged ropes,
      cables, hoses — lost all touch
       contact with the oft-reckless scouts of the deep,
        fearing breaks in the line. . . .
      But the divers resurfaced, always,
     dizzied and pale, yet resurrected
    in airspace, their vertigo more a spirit malaise
   than the bends, or body
stress. . . . *Oh what man can abide fathomless depths,*
unscaleable heights? . . . Here, the water table,
 a natural hidden reservoir,
  can be struck anyplace by drills
   boring down: this whole country a cornucopia
    of freshwater springs!
   This land a crater-gouged, a miles-long-
  drill-shafted . . . Oh, no quarrels
 have I! Squatting, I cup my hand, to scoop up palmed
  ladlefuls of water
from a mountain spring running past our legs, even
 at this height — my small gulps a nonverbal yes. Slurp yes
  to her fervid praise of Jamaica's
   watergods. Slurp yes to oasis fever
    in her eyes. Eyes' glitter signals my hand-to-mouth
     speech strikes home — so I
    sink to all fours, lower my face
     to the stream: lap and quaff great drafts
      of her country's free ambrosias (a mutt in heat stroke) . . .
  She, warming to the task,
charts the lineaments of each famed watercourse
  and its tributaries. She hails, in turn, each river
   God's, or Demon's, splendor —
    that amalgam of myth and historic
     peaks . . . *The Past*

5.

So begins her recitation of high water marks: *El Rio Bueno.*
  A broth of mud-
 blackened waters. Mud-opaque. Cows of perennial generations
  of cattle ranches

rim its shores, putrid-smelling thrice-yearly with manure
and strewn disembowelments, innards of slaughter fouling
its crusty banks.
In her thirty-six years of ambles to and from
Falmouth's

open market, the piquant gallery of cows cheered her twice-
daily crossovers
of the stagnant Rio Bueno. Wading across the shallow ford
through drugged currents,
while she balanced the tall broad wicker basket (empty
or full) on her cranium, hefting sacks of potatoes
or bales of feather
down with equal aplomb and grace, she'd passed
thousands

of grazing cows, munching riverside sedge and tall grasses.
Stalled in mid passage,
her figure motionless like the sluggish waters, she observed —
with gay painterly eye —
the vivid assortment of shades and colors, a blotched
and mottled pattern of cattle hides shifting from year
to year. She loved
the droopy ruminant procession, allured,
equally,

by purebred cacao-berry-brown bulls and heifers, or by calico
mongrel bull-oxen,
whether piebald black patches on white, or white on black
(the mix of dark
and light so blended, in many hides, who could say which
was the dominant shade?) . . . One day, absently noting
the interplay
between cows and their reflected images,
she woke

to epiphany! The mudblack ink scumming the surface, a light-
impervious film,
was a great leveler: all cattle — sepia, tan, or piebald —
chomping the scrub
of the riverbanks, saw ghost white twins of their heads
and flanks in the river's mud mirror. Their tails wagged

                    white flares, cud-
            chewing muzzles whitely ablaze. In Rio
                Bueno's

    black mirror, all cows are white moons. Where the river muck feeds
            into the wide bay
        of Falmouth Harbor, the whole vast half-moon expanse turns
                mud, mud, mud! — far out
        to sea . . . Why Rio Bueno, I ask: *apt name for mudslime*
            inferno of stinks? Oh, *good for local traders,* she scoffs!
                Named by Spaniards,
            in early days of Spanish rule. No shipments
                hijacked,

    ever, by English pirates, sickened by pestilential odors. . . .
            The many rivers,
        nearing the seacoast, converge in the common mouth of Duns
            River Falls as spokes
        of a wheel merge in the hub, or spread fingers of a glove
            sewn in the palm cloth . . .
                            The Martha Brae River, frothing
                a personality
            as vivid as its Anglican name, sizzles
                and foams

    and whitecaps around rocky breakwaters spaced, at wide intervals,
            from its mountain-top
        source to the falls: the last blowup in unstoppable melee
            of whitewater flareups,
        all fracas and blustery of temperament. In her baptismal
            dousing, it is rumored, many a thief and pillager
                was reborn
            civic hero, or citizen reformer: Gods,
                like humans,

    after repeated dunkings, might change coats, or colors; underworld
            demons and demigods
        hatched into Apollos, Neptunes, or Jupiters . . . Captain Morgan,
            pirate-czar who robbed,
        monthly, galleons of the Spaniards and beat upriver
            retreats over Martha Brae's stormiest currents, flying

≈ 168

    the rapids upstream,
   always eluded the Spanish gunboat fleets
    in pursuit

and fell in love with the River Goddess: Morgan, once a shipwrecked
    castaway, master
 of escape routes and princely of fugitives, mated — imagine it! —
   to volatile Martha, she,
bordered with inlets and rimmed with secret harbors,
  all havens for hideaways . . . Legend has it, the Spanish
    colonists — driven
   hence — fled to Cuba, minus their treasures,
    whereupon

skipper Morgan returned from three years obscurity and exile,
    transfigured by love's
lavings, love's wavelets and eddies, love's sandbars and algae
    and starfish. Sporting
a forty-months gray beard, shoulders hidden in cascades
  of curled locks, he emerged the people's statesman —
   a landslide victory,
   avalanche of votes. A reformed pirate elected
    Governor! . . .

Today, his jilted paramour, vivacious to all who saddle her
    bucking wave-crests, wafts
and floats the daily teams of rafts: cloth-lined rubber balloons,
    bamboo and osier-woven
 log frames, old hollow wooden doors, solo daredevils
  on driftwood timbers, a few surfboard buffs, canoeists
    and paddleboard one-man
   dugouts; the rafters a cosmopolitan mix
    of natives

and foreigners, who turn out in greater numbers each year for raft
    river-speedways. The racers'
stretch of whitewater rapids, like an Olympics skiers' trail
    beset with hazards, starts
in a mountain pool, the first runoff a wide mild falls
  giving a sharp launching boost to contestants. Many capsize,
   a few climbing ashore

        for treatment of wounds, or repairs of their craft.
           They drag

the rafts by ropes from the bank to the starters' plateau for second
        launchings (third or fourth,
    it may be), repeated capsizers disqualified after four failed
        tries. No races today!
But we can see flying specks and dotted wafers bobbing,
    at intervals, on strips of the river's ribboning zigzags
        visible in distant
        foothills . . . The next wide band, glittery waterway,
        its course

a natural roller-coaster of switchbacks, loops, abrupt dips,
        vanishings in tunnels,
detours around rock colossi, swerves into hidden recess,
        sheltered nook, inlet:
Rio Nuevo, site of the last cycle of battles,
    the fugitive half-crippled Spanish armada chased
        by British gunboats
      hiding for weeks at a stretch in obscure coves,
        camouflaged

by webworks of palmetto thatch shrewdly woven into sheets,
        tentlike shrouds
covering the beached vessels, while scattered remnants
        of Latins combined forces —
slowly, they mobilized for a last Kamikaze counter-
    offensive. The tribe of survivors, following the carnage,
        fled, via the nearby
        Green Grotto Caves (thereafter, dubbed *Runaway Caves*),
        to Cuba,

hurriedly patching together rafts from salvaged timbers hauled
        underground, chunks
        of mast and rigging (ropes, chains, charred sails) torn
        from the hull carcass
of wrecked galleons, bits and pieces sewn into patchwork
    sails for the Cuba-aimed rafts. Crawling from the cave burrows
        at dead of night
        like grave robbers or ghouls, skulking to the shaded
        river mouth

(midsummer overcast: the night moonless, starless), they drifted,
				downwind, across the bay
	to open sea, slipping past the arrogant Anglo-captains,
				who, grown lackadaisical
	and cocky in their conquest, supposed they'd exterminated
		every last Spanish patriot, thus allowing the small-scale
				downisland
		exodus . . .
					Vamanos! — the last of Jamaica's
		Spanish-

speaking minority: the year 1658. . . . One hundred years passage.
			A fork-branch of Rio
	Nuevo borders on a wealthy sugar plantation, the owner
			a deposed Voodoo
	Queen — exiled from Haiti — taking on a succession
		of lovers, each chosen from jampacked stable of slaves.
			For two decades,
			fantastic rumors burgeon, tales of Obeah
			murders

by riverside, the ritual dismemberment of each slave lover
			when she tired of his charms,
	or sexual favors.
				River burials of the corpse. Burials
			of severed black limbs,
	severed members. Slavewomen horrified by swollen flesh
		geranium, surf-bobbed to shore following storm. The intact
			puffy genital —
		it is believed — seeks vengeance! Self-exhumed
			from its grave

of water, it pursues the Haitian white witch — she strangled,
			at last, in a slave
	revolt . . .
				The liberated slaves found sanctuary, brief haven,
			in the Runaway Caves.
	Months later, after the lynch mobs and search parties quit
		the hunt, the fugitives dug deep pit-traps for their pursuers
			and slunk away upriver,
			hugging the furrowed banks back to the river's
			mountain-peak

source, and founding their own secluded hamlets, a permanent
       freedmen's colony,
   their heirs locked in the mind-set of eternal revolt against
       the tyrant witchmistress.
   Their cousins would claim squatters' rights on plantations
    now owned and run by offspring of former slaves, the Rosehall
       Manor House left
      standing: a haunted memorial to the defunct
         slave era. . . .

6.

Now, tuned for last, she chants of the broadest whitewater artery,
       if most distant from us —
       the aristocrat! *Great River*.
   The main channel a lunging basin catching runoffs
    from two mountain ranges, its long quicksilver stretches —
ribboning from mountaintop
      to seacoast — are interrupted by two sharp bends.
       Torrents overflow the banks, flooding
     pastures and plantations for miles on either side,
following storms. The worst recent storm, more river-
   choking than the hurricanes — she recalls —
   was ten months back. Downpour gush

massive and prolonged, flashfloods rampant, the risen maelstrom
      carried livestock (hoofs
        upturned, pointing skyward), whole
   shithouses intact, bobbing upright like phone booths
  afloat; just-cut stalks of harvested cane juggled and whipped
about the swirling surface,
      tens of thousands of stalks bounced on their tails
       like pickupstix, many hurled spearlike,
        impaling bulls, horses, sheep, or human passersby —
as tornado driven straws pierce barnsides, fence
   posts. Banana sheds, thatchroofs torn off,
   were catapulted on shore rocks,

upchucking their contents, countless bananas radiating in tiers
       around the bound stalks

        interlaced in sheaves, now stripped
of their green and yellow curved-finger-fruit thousands,
hundreds ripping off per second, weightless in the fierce gales
as leaves or rose petals;
        banana sludge plastering the highways, windshields
        and sides of passing trucks, bridge cables
        and steel-frame crossed slats with shredded green peels
and yellow citrus splotches: tobacco leaves, mud, limes
        and pimento berries painting all exposed
        surface of the seashore

in a continuous banana-base fruit collage. She hymns a total-
        environment canvas
        as Jackson Pollock abstract! . . .
Chickens and turkeys, by the coop-bushelfuls, spinning
like tops, exposed wattle necks and pipecleaner jointed legs
poking above the surface,
        by turns; mixed eggyolk sprinkles and wind-whipped
        shellbit hails gorging the atmosphere
        of breathers like fine silica in the lungs of bauxite
miners. . . . She reports this comic storm of organic
        tidbits and particles, observed firsthand,
        she taking cover behind

a firm-rooted royal palm, the river-borne world of shrapnel
        debris roaring past . . .
        She sees puffballs of chickenwire
rolling and somersaulting like mammoth tumbleweeds
over the locked melee of river-jam whipped contents; her eye
so bewitched by the carnival
        display of sandwiched shapes and colors, dreamlike,
        fear and all thought of danger falls away.
        She feels absurdly free! She is an eggshell, yolkstained,
dancing in spray tinged by the late low sun's rose
        pink glaze, and for moments, happily, she
        prays to be stripped of her rind,

her heavy shell of skin and flesh. She would trade her frail bones
        for the frailer curled
        half-shell of the egg, buffeted
by wind and spray, so happy in the topsy-turvy

   dance — spinning on itself without cease. . . . But the bottom
of the dream bursts upwards!
    The mainstays of the scene — walls of a theatre
    on opposite sides of the stage —
   collapse at once. No, she makes an effort over her eyes
to transcribe the optical mixup erupted into view . . .
    The two bridge ends, slowly caving in, slant
    to the center. Cracks zigzag.

The foundations, at both sides, buckle, cement blocks shaken
    loose at the top, tossed
    this way and that like cardboard cubes.
   Caught in a whirlpool below, many roofs are tangled
in a coil — outhouses, chicken coops, banana sheds, sugar
cane and tobacco huts —
    each roof typified by a unique design, but outlines
    blurred in the hodgepodge jumble
   of eaves, split rafters, ridgepoles, loosed nails, sheet tin
and zinc squares . . . All are mud-glued in a vast hoop-shape!
    Cartwheeling like the blade of a giant chainsaw
    into the bridge midsection,

it hurtles against frame and suspended roadway. The third charge —
    adding chunks of concrete
    and timbers to the roof cartwheel's
   combined mass — heaves the bridgepiles inward at both
extremities, and, in less than a flicked eye-blink, bursts
the bridge-frame at the center,
    the two severed halves of highway jackknifed upwards
    (now she'd recalled seeing segments
   of Miami causeway, upraised in slow motion, those lips
of black asphalt sensuously parted to give berth
    to tall masts of the approaching sailboat
    in a Florida film travelog),

leaving a trucksized gap in the middle, the long bauxite-heaped
    truck, its hill of ore
    forming a smallish cone-shaped peak,
   still intact, visible a few yards above the trailer top.
    The twelve-wheel steel chassis horizontal yet, as if parachuted
from above, slowgliding, drops

through the widening slot. It caps the mound of flotsam
and is swept, whirling, out to sea.
   The driver, his expression dazed but head and shoulders unbudged
behind the steering wheel, switches on windshield wipers,
   blinking *hazard* lights, turn signal, and rotates
   lit spotlight beam — his eyes aglow,

expectant... In his trance, the dashboard combination of gadgetry
      should quickly correct
      the disordered highway cosmos...
   A thin trail of exhaust smoke, spiralling higher
   and higher from his diesel smokestack, is starkly visible, still,
long after the truck — tumbled
      from the heap — has plunged into the sea... Fear shatters
      the swollen bubble of her fantasia
      of images. She runs from riverbank to high ground, for safety
from ravaging floodwaters, never once glancing back
   over her shoulder to survey aftershocks
   of the bridge dismantlement....

7.

            At daybreak, thick bags of provisions
                    and paratroopers
                     could be seen
                    dropping from a fleet
                   of giant metallic wasps
             (*helicopters*, she heard them named
               later that mornng), hundreds
             of homeless wayfarers arriving —
                    from all parishes
                 of countryside — to receive
                     doled handouts
              from the U.S. Marines. The peasants
            and farmers, I knew from her story's tone,

              were more bountiful in their thankyous
                    than the beefy troops
                      who meted out
                  my country's "care packets"

and Red Cross supplies. *Manna.*
Her eyes now grant *me* thanks, unearned,
on behalf of my fellow
countrymen in spiffy uniforms,
that militia
of aiders . . . Later that morning,
the choppers
dangling steel hooks from chains, bunched
in squads of three and four, dragged the dozen,

or so, jigsaw chunks of metal framework
and pavement amalgam
topped with slabs
of marl-based tarmac (the latter
resembling the ruins
of mammoth blackboards) from Great River's
debris-clogged basin. One by one,
the airborne demolitions crew grappled
and carted away
one-hundred-ton wedges and jagged
pie slices
of dismembered bridge, loading the webbed
girders and steel-beam sections in teetery heaps

stacked on the beach adjacent to fallen
bridge pylons. The high-piled
units, towering
over nearby royal palms —
asway in moderate winds — seemed
a child's prank of balancing Tinkertoys
or Erector sets . . . Some pilots,
endeared to local pals, returned, months
later, to construct
the new bridge, working side-by-side
with native crews,
humming reggae tunes, and bandying tales
of the storm that unleashed Great River's Demon. . . .

www.ingramcontent.com/pod-product-compliance
Lightning Source LLC
Chambersburg PA
CBHW011952150426
43196CB00019B/2917